TONAL AND RHYTHMIC PRINCIPLES

Jazz Improvisation I

REVISED AND ENLARGED EDITION

John Mehegan

Watson-Guptill Publications/New York

Amsco Publications
New York/London/Sydney

To Linda
Tara and Gretchen
Lucille and Ron

Revised edition published 1984 in New York by Watson-Guptill Publications,
a division of Billboard Publications, Inc.,
1515 Broadway, New York, N.Y. 10036

Exclusive distributors to the Music Trade

Music Sales Corporation
24 E. 22 Street
New York, N.Y. 10010

Music Sales Limited
8/9 Frith Street
London W1V 5TZ

Music Sales Pty Limited
27 Clarendon Street
Artarmon
Sydney NSW 2064

Library of Congress Catalog Card Number: 84-50368

Manufactured in U.S.A.

3 4 5 6/90 89 88

CONTENTS

PREFACE

There has long been a need for a sharp, clear, wise textbook which would once and for all codify and delineate that elusive procedure known as jazz improvisation. Of course, no improvisation can ever be explained down to its roots; therein lies the mystery and joy of spontaneous creation. And any improvisation will vary greatly in proportion to talent, mood, colleagues and endless personal factors.

Still, there *is* a basis to improvisation of any kind: a coupling of traditions and techniques. And that basis *can* be explained, difficult though it may be. I suppose it is this difficulty that has prevented such a book from having been written heretofore; but at last there is a Johnny Mehegan who has the ability to do it. He has that peculiar combination of abilities which is absolutely necessary for such an endeavor: academic and scholarly knowledge (and insight and interest), plus an immense practical knowledge (and insight and interest) born of long years of simply doing it himself and teaching others to do it. I am proud to be able to write this preface to what I am sure will be a highly important and valuable publication.

Leonard Bernstein

INTRODUCTION

This book is an attempt to describe the process that occurs when a jazz musician improvises. This process is not a mysterious and esoteric rite arbitrarily enacted without discipline or precise knowledge. Rather, it is a concise application of logical and comprehensible musical concepts, which attains amazing heights of expression when utilized in conjunction with a trained and imaginative talent.

To do anything well, some intuitive knowledge of the material at hand is required; this intuition we often call talent. But talent without knowledge and hard facts is nothing. Talent does not need to be described; the facts do need to be set forth and that is the function of this book.

This book analyzes the basic musical facts utilized by every jazz musician from Buddy Bolden to Dizzy Gillespie. These facts, strangely enough, can be expressed in the eternal trinity of all music (1), Melody; (2) Harmony; (3) Rhythm.

1. Melody. Each jazz generation develops its own repertoire which best suits its own specific ideas of rhythm (time) and harmony (chord changes). The melodies referred to in this book are more adaptable for modern interpretation. However, the basic materials of this book are adaptable and essential to all jazz styles.

2. Harmony. Jazz harmony is diatonic or major scale harmony found in the mainstream of classical music from 1600 to 1900. In other words, jazz harmony is classical harmony following the identical rules and conventions found in a Bach fugue, a Mozart sonata, a Brahms rhapsody.

The confusion in this area has resulted from the single fact that jazz musicians have, by nature, been gifted people whose sole concern has been to play and to leave it at that. Analyses and descriptive material have been avoided by jazz musicians and have, in general, been left to popular theorists who possess little insight into the real structure of the music.

When the need to communicate with each other arises, or on being pressed to describe the process of their music, jazz musicians have turned to the makeshift spelling of lettered chords found in sheet music as a means of expression despite the fact that chord letters can offer only a careless approximation of what occurs in a musical function. Today, this makeshift knowledge is not enough to meet the theoretical and technical levels existing in jazz. The young jazz musician can no longer leave the basis of his knowledge to such idle devices as have prevailed in the past.

The use of chord letters among musicians may seem strange when one considers that an organized method of spelling any musical function has existed for some two hundred years — Figured Bass. This is the first serious attempt to apply figured bass to jazz. Using figured bass, the jazz musician can for the first time correctly and completely indicate his music with precision. An irony here is that the jazz musician plays out of one ear and talks out of the other. No jazz musician thinks of lettered chords when he is playing; he hears interval steps based on the distance between one chord and another. Distance can best be described by number. In other words, the jazz musician plays by the natural system of figured bass. In describing this music, it is reasonable that the same system should be used.

For instance, in the problem of transposition and modulation so important to the jazz musician, letters break down completely because they can refer only to one key at a time. Of course it is possible to work out twelve spellings for the twelve keys, but with figured bass one spelling using numbers can be used for twelve keys, since the relationships in one key obtain for all other keys.

This symmetrical system of relating the keys to each other must eventually be adopted by jazz musicians as a means of meeting the increasing demands for communication and teaching. Top jazz musicians today acknowledge the need for this new language as a means of bringing jazz into the family of the arts on a permanent and secure basis.

3. Rhythm. This is a projected four-volume series in which we will learn first what to do (tonal) and then how to do it (rhythmic). Book II will trace the history of the improvised line (the heart of the jazz matter) from 1900 to the present day. Specific examples will enable the student to develop his own sense of lineal harmony.

It is in the area of rhythm that the jazz musician has made his most magnificent achievement. It is these rhythmic qualities that have enchanted people all over the world and have become the universal symbol of the sound of jazz.

There is no counterpart in classical music for the unique rhythmic elements in jazz. This combination of rhythmic elements can best be described as a form of florid counterpoint involving three levels of time played simultaneously:

Eighth-note—first level;
Half-note—second level;
Quarter-note—third level.

Here is the catalyst that converts conventional harmonic elements into the excitement of a jazz performance. The function of this book is to explore fully the tonal material which forms the basis for this rhythm.

Problems of style are beyond the scope of this volume and will be treated in Volumes II, III, and IV.

In writing this book, the author has kept in mind the large cross section of the musical public which has comprised his students for over twenty-five years—professionals, aspiring semiprofessionals, dedicated amateurs and the Sunday pianist. All have experienced the need to supplement their talents with an orderly body of musical facts.

There seems no point in deprecating previous attempts to assess these facts. Two streams of endeavor have been pursuing slowly converging lines of activity for the past twenty years—the improviser on the one hand, the theorist on the other. Until recently, these two factions have trod their separate paths, often with mutual hostility and certainly with misunderstanding.

Today the art form has evolved to a point at which the improviser and the theorist can calmly exchange their views.

"Popular" piano methods are completely outmoded in terms of modern music. Most of these methods are based upon antiquated ragtime concepts (swing bass) that have no resemblance to the realities of piano as it is played today. This book is an initial attempt to bring to all who love jazz some understanding of the beauties of this great art.

It is hoped that this book will be a further contribution to the growing literature of jazz which already bears witness to its significance as a vital art form.

The author wishes to express his indebtedness to the following whose efforts in behalf of the revised edition of this book were so valuable: Els Sincebaugh, Linda Pomerantz, Robin White Goode, Ginny Croft, Ellen Greene, Richard Grossman, Clarence Foy, Richard Rodgers, Dr. Albert Sirmay, Paul Rosen, Norman Monath, George Elber.

SECTION I

LESSON 1.

The Scale-tone Seventh Chords

The harmony of popular music and jazz is based on the diatonic or major scale (Fig 1). Each of the twelve scales is a frame forming the harmonic system.

Fig. 1. Scale of C.

Diatonic harmony moves in two directions: Horizontal (Fig. 1) and Vertical (Fig. 2).

Fig. 2.

By combining these two movements using the root (one), third, fifth and seventh, we derive the scale-tone seventh chords in the key of C (Fig. 3).

Fig. 3.

Chords of less than a seventh are insufficient for jazz; chords of more than a seventh will be treated in Volume IV.

Fig. 4 illustrates the scale of G, Fig. 5, the scale-tone seventh chords in the key of G.

Fig. 4.

Fig. 5.

In Figs. 3 and 5, the scale-tone seventh chords are derived by combining the following tones of each scale:

Chord	Scale-tones			
I	1	3	5	7
II	2	4	6	1
III	3	5	7	2
IV	4	6	1	3
V	5	7	2	4
VI	6	1	3	5
VII	7	2	4	6

The ideal register for the bottom notes of these chords in the left hand is as follows:

Bass line motion and the register requirements of melodies will sometimes force the left hand down to low G (see below).

In extreme conditions of register disorientation, the student may be forced to move the melody up an octave and leave the middle C area to the left hand.

In two-handed drill, the right hand appears in the octave immediately above the left hand.

Fig. 6. Scale of F — Scale-tone seventh chords.

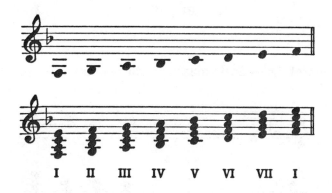

Fig. 7. Scale of D — Scale-tone seventh chords.

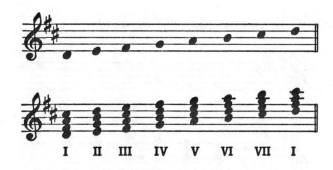

Fig. 8. Scale of B♭ — Scale-tone seventh chords.

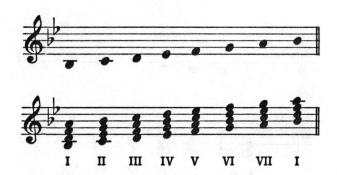

Fig. 9. Scale of A — Scale-tone seventh chords.

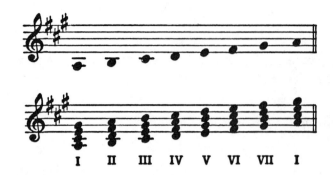

Fig. 10. Scale of E♭ — Scale-tone seventh chords.

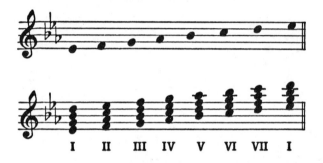

Fig. 11. Scale of E — Scale-tone seventh chords.

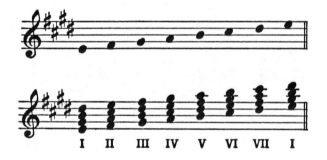

Fig. 12. Scale of A♭ — Scale-tone seventh chords.

Fig. 13. Scale of B — Scale-tone seventh chords.

I II III IV V VI VII I

Fig. 14. Scale of D♭ — Scale-tone seventh chords.

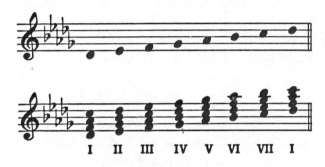

I II III IV V VI VII I

Fig. 15. Scale of F♯ — Scale-tone seventh chords.

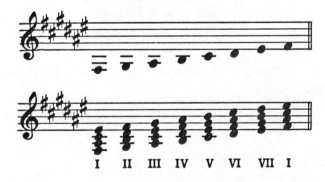

I II III IV V VI VII I

Fig. 16. Scale of G♭ — Scale-tone seventh chords.

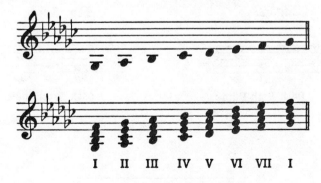

I II III IV V VI VII I

NOTE: It is important for the student to deal with the spelling of both Figs. 15 and 16.

DRILL: Practice the scale-tone seventh chords in the twelve keys — both hands.

During this period of his development the student should strive to keep his eyes on the keyboard rather than on the printed page.

LESSON 2.

Intervals

Intervals represent the distance of one scale-tone to another. Fig. 1 illustrates the intervals in the scale of C.

Fig. 1.

C to D is a Second
C to E is a Third
C to F is a Fourth
C to G is a Fifth
C to A is a Sixth
C to B is a Seventh
C to C is an Octave

Intervals fall into two groups: Primary — 4th, 5th, 8th; Secondary — 2nd, 3rd, 6th, 7th.

If a Fourth, Fifth or Octave falls in the scale of the Root, it is Perfect (P) (Fig. 2).

If it is lowered — Diminished (o) (Fig. 3).

If it is raised — Augmented (+) (Fig. 4).

Fig. 2.　　　　　Fig. 3.

P4th P5th P8th　　　o4th o5th o8th

Fig. 4.

+4th　+5th　+8th

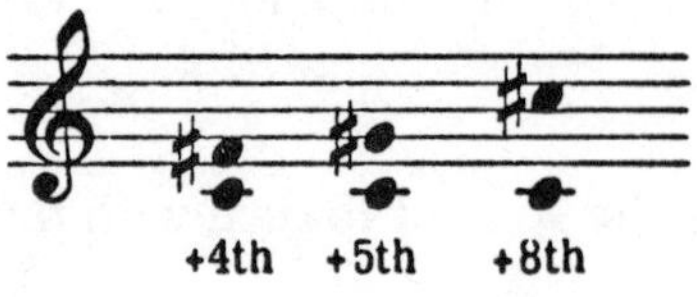

If a Second, Third, Sixth or Seventh falls in the scale of the Root, it is major (M) (Fig. 5). If it is lowered — minor (m) (Fig. 6).

Fig. 5.

M2nd M3rd M6th M7th

Fig. 6.

m2nd m3rd m6th m7th

Symbol key:

P — Perfect
o — Diminished
+ — Augmented
M — Major
m — Minor

These rules apply to all twelve scales. Fig. 7 illustrates the scale-tone seventh chords in the key of C.

Fig. 7.

I   II   III   IV   V   VI   VII   I

By applying the interval rules, we derive the following combinations:

Based on the scale of C, the I chord contains M3, P5, M7
Based on the scale of D, the II chord contains, m3, P5, m7
Based on the scale of E, the III chord contains m3, P5, m7
Based on the scale of F, the IV chord contains M3, P5, M7
Based on the scale of G, the V chord contains M3, P5, m7
Based on the scale of A, the VI chord contains m3, P5, m7
Based on the scale of B, the VII chord contains m3, o5, m7

NOTE: The student should be careful not to confuse the "key" of C with the "scales" of C, D, E, F, G, A and B used to determine the intervals for each chord. The chords belong to the "key" of C; their intervals are determined on the basis of the major "scale" of each root.

15

We have seen how this is applied to the key of C. *It is also true in all keys*. Thus, in all keys:

CHORD	INTERVALS		
	3	5	7
I	M	P	M
II	m	P	m
III	m	P	m
IV	M	P	M
V	M	P	m
VI	m	P	m
VII	m	o	m

DRILL: Continue to play the scale-tone seventh chords in 12 keys. Study interval steps in 12 scales (as in Fig. 1). Memorize interval combinations for each scale-tone seventh chord.

LESSON 3.

Chord Qualities

We may now proceed to the chord values or qualities formed by the interval combinations in Lesson 2.

The following outline illustrates the interval combinations, their scale position and chord qualities for *all* twelve keys.

COMBINATION			POSITION	QUALITY
3	5	7		
M	P	M	I, IV	Major Seventh Chord
M	P	m	V	Dominant Seventh Chord
m	P	m	II, III, VI	Minor Seventh Chord
m	o	m	VII	Half-diminished Seventh Chord

In other words, in *any key*

The I chord is always MAJOR
The II chord is always MINOR
The III chord is always MINOR
The IV chord is always MAJOR
The V chord is always DOMINANT
The VI chord is always MINOR
The VII chord is always HALF-DIMINISHED

There is one chord used extensively in jazz harmony which does not appear naturally in any key — the *diminished* seventh chord. This chord may be formed at any point on the keyboard by building an interval combination of m3, o5, o7. The o7 interval is lowered twice from its scale position and is written in Fig. 1, as a M6 for convenience.

Fig. 1.

Co   Fo   Go

We now have the five qualities or kinds of chords necessary for jazz harmony. The following table is the complete Quality Series with the interval combinations:

INTERVALS 3 5 7	QUALITY POSITIONS	QUALITY
M P M	I, IV	Major Seventh Chord
M P m	V	Dominant Seventh Chord
m P m	II, III, VI	Minor Seventh Chord
m o m	VII	Half-diminished Seventh Chord
m o o		Diminished Seventh Chord

DRILL: Thoroughly memorize the qualities of the scale-tone seventh chords. Memorize the interval combinations for the five qualities. Practice the scale-tone seventh chords in 12 keys — both hands — in the following patterns:

II - V - I.
I - VI - II - V - I.
I - IV - VII - III - VI - II - V - I.

LESSON 4.

Altered Scale-tone Seventh Chords

Symbol key:

M — Major Chord
x — Dominant Chord
m — Minor Chord
φ — Half-diminished Chord
o — Diminished Chord

Jazz harmony is extremely chromatic and it is important to be able to build any quality at any point in the scale. This requires *altering* from one quality to another. The following table describes the Alteration Series from the four natural qualities (M, x, m, φ).

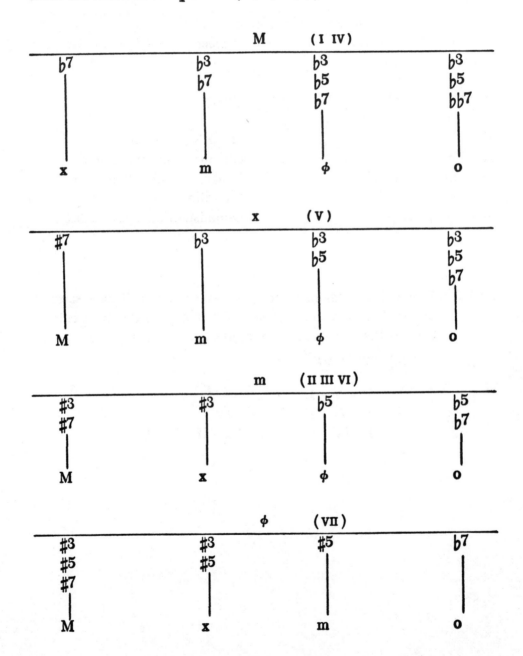

	M (I IV)		
♭7	♭3	♭3	♭3
	♭7	♭5	♭5
		♭7	♭♭7
x	m	φ	o

	x (V)		
♯7	♭3	♭3	♭3
		♭5	♭5
			♭7
M	m	φ	o

	m (II III VI)		
♯3	♯3	♭5	♭5
♯7			♭7
M	x	φ	o

	φ (VII)		
♯3	♯3	♯5	♭7
♯5	♯5		
♯7			
M	x	m	o

18

The first group of this series reads as follows:

To alter a Major chord to a Dominant — flat the seventh;

To alter a Major chord to a Minor — flat the third and flat the seventh;

To alter a Major chord to a Half-diminished chord, flat the third, flat the fifth and flat the seventh;

To alter a Major chord to a Diminished, flat the third, flat the fifth and double-flat the seventh.

The remaining series read in the same manner. The symbols for these alterations are as follows:

I means I Major (understood);

Ix means I Dominant;

Im means I Minor;

Iφ means I Half-diminished;

Io means I Diminished.

These chords are illustrated in Fig. 1.

Fig. 1.

I   Ix   Im   Iφ   Io

DRILL: Practice the following alterations in 12 keys:

Ix - Im - Iφ - Io   IIM - IIx - IIφ - IIo

IIIM - IIIx - IIIφ - IIIo   IVx - IVm - IVφ - IVo

VM - Vm - Vφ - Vo   VIM - VIx - VIφ - VIo

VIIM - VIIx - VIIm - VIIo

LESSON 5.

Chromatic and Altered-chromatic Scale-tone Seventh Chords

Any scale-tone chord may be raised or lowered chromatically by sharping or flatting each note in the chord one semitone (m2). Thus, in Fig. 1, II in the key of C can be raised or lowered by simply indicating ♯II or ♭II. Since II in any key is Minor, ♯II and ♭II will also be Minor.

Fig. 1.

II   ♯II   ♭II

19

It is also possible to alter any scale-tone chord before raising or lowering the chord. Thus, Fig 2 illustrates:

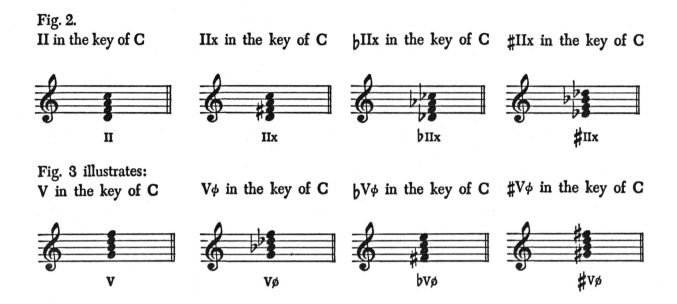

Fig. 2.

II in the key of C   IIx in the key of C   ♭IIx in the key of C   ♯IIx in the key of C

II   IIx   ♭IIx   ♯IIx

Fig. 3 illustrates:
V in the key of C   V∅ in the key of C   ♭V∅ in the key of C   ♯V∅ in the key of C

V   V∅   ♭V∅   ♯V∅

The devices of Chromaticism and Alteration are essential to jazz harmony and must be thoroughly mastered by the student in all 12 keys.

DRILL: Play the following chromatic scale-tone chords in 12 keys:

♯I - ♭II - ♯II - ♭III - ♭V - ♯V - ♭VI - ♯VI - ♭VII

Although ♯V and ♭VI appear on the same tone, their quality will vary since V is dominant and VI is minor. On the other hand, ♯II and ♭III will be of the same quality since both II and III are minor chords.

Play the following altered chromatic scale-tone chords in 12 keys:

♭IIx - ♯IIo - ♭IIIx - ♭IIIo - ♯IVm - ♯IVo - ♭Vm
♭V∅ - ♯Vo - ♭VIx - ♭VI∅ - ♯VIo - ♭VIIx - ♭VIIm - ♭VIIo

LESSON 6.

The Sixty Chords

Jazz harmony utilizes *five qualities*. We have learned in Lessons 4 and 5 that these qualities can be applied at any point on the keyboard. There are twelve tones in the octave, each capable of supporting the five qualities. Thus, jazz harmony employs a Sixty Chord System. Fig. 1 illustrates these sixty chords.

Fig. 1.* The Sixty Chord System.

DRILL: Practice the five qualities on twelve tones with both hands. These series should be played without constant reference to the printed page. The student must develop automatic knowledge of the keyboard on three levels: 1. Muscular (hands); 2. Visual (eyes); 3. Auditory (ears).

Jazz playing must be done without reference to written music; learning the sixty chords automatically is the first step in this development.

NOTE*: Transferring to sharps on m, ∅ and o is for ease in "spelling" these chords. Also, C♯m belongs to B, A and E — all sharp keys; C♯∅ belongs to D — a sharp key; C♯o belongs to no key but is most easily spelled in this way.

21

SECTION II

LESSON **7.**

Key of C

We can now proceed to the application of the sixty chord system to the popular song — the basic repertoire of jazz. Fig. 1 is a model of the procedure to be followed. The melody (an original melody) has been transferred from sheet music to manuscript paper leaving a bass clef for the Roman numerals.

Fig. 1.

See Fig. 6. 23

One chord to a bar indicates that the chord is held for four beats.

Two chords to a bar indicates that the first chord is played on the first beat, the second chord on the third beat.

Three chords to a bar are accompanied by wedges (*see* Fig. 2) indicating best values.

Four chords to a bar indicates that each chord falls on one beat in the measure.

Fig. 2.

SUSPENSION. The dominant and minor chords are occasionally suspended for purposes of melodic adjustment or harmonic suspense. The suspensions are easily made and affect the dominant and minor chords as follows:

CHORD	SUSPENSION	SYMBOL	
x	sharp third	$V^{\sharp 3}$	Fig. 3
m	double-sharp seventh	$II^{\sharp\sharp 7}$	Fig. 4
m	sharp seventh	$II^{\sharp 7}$	Fig. 5

Fig. 3.   Fig. 4.   Fig. 5.

The minor suspension may involve only the sharp seventh (Fig. 5) or both (Figs. 4 & 5).

The dominant suspension is known generally as the Eleventh chord. It often appears in sheet music as the suspended fourth.

ADDED SIXTH CHORD. The major and minor chords employ the Added Sixth either for melodic adjustment or for a feeling of finality. In either case, the seventh is omitted and the major sixth of the scale of the root is added to the three remaining tones (*see* Fig. 6).

Fig. 6.

The student should be aware that the following copyrighted tunes appear with a title and a chord chart. Any reproduction of the melodies of these songs is strictly forbidden by copyright law.

It should be noted that the author is not allowed to reproduce melodies for the songs appearing in this and successive volumes. The student must have access to sheet music, folios, or "fake" books in order to structure the lessons properly.

Fig. 7 is a bass line for "Fools Rush In." Transfer the melody from sheet music to manuscript paper using alternate staves so that the Roman numerals (bass line) may be added beneath the melody, as in Fig. 1 of this lesson.

Fig. 7.

II$^{\sharp\sharp7}$ II$^{\sharp7}$ / II IVo / III / VI / II / $\flat$IIx / I / $\sharp$Io / II / V$^{\sharp3}$ /

I^{+6} / VI / IIx$^{\flat5}$ IIx / VI $\flat$IIIo / II / V IV III $\flat$IIIx /

II$^{\sharp\sharp7}$ II$^{\sharp7}$ / II IVo / III / VI / II$^{\sharp\sharp7}$ II$^{\sharp7}$ / II V / $\flat$VIIx /

VIx / II III / IVm $\flat$VIIx / III / VI / II / V$^{\sharp3}$ / I^{+6} / I^{+6} //

FOOLS RUSH IN—Words by Johnny Mercer, Music by Gus Kahn
  © 1940 (renewed) Warner Bros. Music Corp. All rights reserved.
  Used by permission.

LESSON 8.

Key of G

The following is a bass line for "Nice Work if You Can Get It." Transfer the melody to manuscript paper, as in Lesson 7.

IIIx $\flat$IIIx / IIx $\flat$IIx / I^{+6} IVx / IIx $\sharp$IIo / III VI /

II III / IV^{+6} V$^{\sharp3}$ / I^{+6} / IIIx $\flat$IIIx / IIx $\flat$IIx / I^{+6} IVx /

IIx $\sharp$IIo / III VI / II III / IV^{+6} V$^{\sharp3}$ / I^{+6}/ VI^{+6} / Im IVx /

VI$^{\sharp\sharp7}$ VI$^{\sharp7}$ / VI $\flat$VIx / Vm^{+6} IIIϕ / VI IIx / II III / IVm V$^{\sharp5}$ /

IIIx $\flat$IIIx / IIx $\flat$IIx / I^{+6} IVx / IIx $\sharp$IIo /

III VI / II III / $\flat$VIIx VIx / II V$^{\sharp3}$ / I^{+6} / I^{+6} //

NICE WORK IF YOU CAN GET IT—George Gershwin and Ira Gershwin
  © 1937 by Chappell & Co., Inc. © renewed.
  International copyright secured. All rights reserved.
  Used by permission.

Key of F

The following is a bass line for "I'm Glad There Is You." Transfer the melody to manuscript paper, as in Lessons 7 and 8.

I / I / Im / Im / II / IVo / III ♭IIIx / II ♭IIx / I II / III ♭IIIo /

II♯♯⁷ II♯⁷ / II V / ♭VIIx♭⁵ / VIx / II V / Vm ♭V / IV / IVm ♭VIIx /

I IV / VIIm ♭VIIx / VI♯♯⁷ VI♯⁷ / VI ♭IIIo / II / ♭IIx / I / I / Im /

Im / II♯♯⁷ II♯⁷ / II IVo / IIIφ / ♭IIIx / II♯♯⁷ II♯⁷ /

II ♭IIx / I⁺⁶ / I⁺⁶ //

Key of D

Since learning to play in twelve keys is so important to jazz improvising, and since the scale-tone seventh chords are as applicable in one key as another, the only thing to be transposed is the melody. Lessons 10, 12, 14, 16, 17, 18 and 19 involve transposition of the melody from one key to another. Failure to transpose these assignments can only prevent the twelve key facility that is necessary. It is impossible to find sheet music of possible jazz tunes written in these keys and, as a result, the transposition technique must be used. The student must keep in mind that avoiding this transposition does not affect the author — it will be the student's loss.

Melodic transposition is best achieved by numbering each melody tone indicating its position in the original key (*see* Fig. 1); then transpose their numerical positions to the new key maintaining the time values (*see* Fig. 2).

Note that melody tones appearing out of the key signature are indicated by adding ♯ or ♭ to the number. Figs. 1 and 2 illustrate this treatment to a fragment of the melody appearing in Lesson 7, Fig. 1.

Fig. 1.

Fig. 2. Transposed to the key of D major.

Fig. 3 is a bass line for "Misty." The sheet music appears in E♭. When transferring the melody, it must be transposed to D major. (*See* explanation above.)

Fig. 3. "Misty."

pick-up

♭IIx♭5 // I VI / Vm Ix / IV / IVm ♭VIIx / III VI / II V / ♭VIIx VIx /

IIx ♭IIx♭5 / I VI / Vm Ix / IV / IVm ♭VIIx / III VI / II ♭IIx / I+6 ♯I /

I+6 VI / Vm♯♯7 Vm♯7 / Vm ♭V / IV Vm / VI II / ♭Vm VIIx /

♭Vm IVx♯♯5 / III ♭IIIx / II ♭IIx♭5 / I VI / Vm Ix / IV / IVm ♭VIIx /

III VI / II V / ♭VIM ♭VIIx / I+6 //

The following table identifies the proper spellings of the inversions appearing in Lessons 11 through 19.

	MAKESHIFT SPELLING	IDENTIFICATION
Lesson 11:	III$^{\sharp\sharp R}_{\sharp 3}$	VIIm$^4_3$
	V$^{\sharp R}_{\flat 7}$	IIIx$^6_5$
	II$^{\sharp\sharp R}_{\sharp 3}$	VI$^4_3$
Lesson 12:	IV$^{\sharp\sharp R}$	VI$_2$
Lesson 14:	I$^{\sharp\sharp R}$	III$_2$
Lesson 15:	IV$^{\sharp\sharp R}$	VI$_2$
	VII$^{\sharp R}$	II$_2$
Lesson 17:	II$^{\sharp\sharp R}_{\sharp 3}$	VI$^4_3$
Lesson 19:	IV$^{\sharp\sharp R}$	VI$_2$
	VII$^{\sharp R}$	II$_2$
	VI$^{\sharp\sharp R}$	I$_2$

LESSON 11.

Key of B♭

The following is a bass line for "Ill Wind," in B♭. Transfer the melody to manuscript paper, as in previous lessons.

see note

I^{+6} IV / VII IIIx$^{\flat 5}$ / III VIx / IVm ♭VIIx / III VI / IIɸ IVɸ / II$^{\sharp\sharp R}_{\sharp 3}$ /

♭IIIx / II / ♭IIx / I^{+6} IV / VII IIIx$^{\flat 5}$ / III VIx / IVm ♭VIIx / III VI /

IIɸ ♭IIx / I^{+6} / ♯I^{+6} / I / IV / IIIx III$^{\sharp\sharp R}_{\sharp 3}$ / Vo V$^{\sharp R}_{\flat 7}$ / III VIx /

III VIx / IIIx III$^{\sharp\sharp R}_{\sharp 3}$ / Vo V$^{\sharp R}_{\flat 7}$ / III VIx / IIɸ ♭IIx / I IV /

VII IIIx$^{\flat 5}$ / III VIx / IVm ♭VIIx / III VI / IIɸ ♭IIx / I^{+6} VIIx /

♭VIIx VI / ♭VIx$^{\sharp 5}$ V / ♭V IV^{+6} / II$^{\sharp\sharp R}_{\sharp 3}$ II / I^{+6} //

Key of A

The following is a bass line for "Moonglow." Transfer the melody to manuscript paper. The sheet music appears in G. The melody must be transposed to A major.

IV / IVm$^{\sharp 7}$ ♭VIIx / III VI / IIx$^{♭5}$ / II$^{\sharp\sharp 7}$ II$^{\sharp 7}$ / II ♭IIx /

IV$^{\sharp\sharp R}$ ♭Vo / IVm^{+6} ♯IVo IV$^{\sharp\sharp R}$ / IV / IVm$^{\sharp 7}$ ♭VIIx / III VI /

IIx$^{♭5}$ / II$^{\sharp\sharp 7}$ II$^{\sharp 7}$ / II ♭IIx / IV$^{\sharp\sharp R}$ ♭Vo / IVm^{+6} ♯IVo IV$^{\sharp\sharp R}$ /

Ix / Ix VIIx ♭VIIx / VIx / III VIx / VI / IIx / II V / Vm Ix /

IV / IVm$^{\sharp 7}$ ♭VIIx / III VI / IIx$^{♭5}$ / II$^{\sharp\sharp 7}$ II$^{\sharp 7}$ / II ♭IIx /

IV$^{\sharp\sharp R}$ ♭Vo / IVm^{+6} ♯IVo IV$^{\sharp\sharp R}$ //

Key of E♭

The following is a bass line for "The Man I Love." Transfer the melody to manuscript paper.

I / Im / IIIφ / ♭IIIx / IIφ / ♭IIx / III ♭IIIx / II ♭IIx /

I / Im / IIIφ / ♭IIIx / IIφ / ♭IIx / I^{+6} ♯I / I^{+6} ♭VIIx /

VI^{+6} ♭Vφ / VIIx ♭VIIx / VI ♭Vφ VIIx / IIIx ♭VIIx / VI^{+6} ♭Vφ /

VIIx IIIx / III ♭IIIx / II ♭IIx / I / Im / IIIφ / ♭IIIx / IIφ /

♭IIx / I^{+6} ♭VIIx / I^{+6} //

Key of E

The following is a bass line for "These Foolish Things." Transfer the melody to manuscript paper, transposing from E♭ to E major.

I^{+6} VI / II ♭IIx / I^{+6} VI / II V / Vm ♭V / IV ♯Io /

IIx / II ♭IIx / I^{+6} VI / II ♭IIx / I^{+6} VI / II V /

Vm ♭V / IV ♯Io / II ♭IIx / I^{+6} VIIx / III^{+6}♭IIø /

♭Vø VIIx / III I$^{♯♯R}$ / ♭IIø Im$^{♯7}$ / VIIm III / VI IIx /

III ♭IIIx / II ♭IIx / I^{+6} VI / II ♭IIx / I^{+6} VI /

II V / Vm ♭V / IV ♯Io / II ♭IIx / I^{+6} //

THESE FOOLISH THINGS—by Strachey, Link, and Marvell

Key of A♭

The following is a bass line for "Spring Is Here." Transfer the melody to manuscript paper.

♭VIx / IV$^{♯♯R}$ / ♭Vø IVx / III VI / Vm Ix / IVm ♭VIIx / IIIø ♭IIIx /

II ♭IIx / I II / III VI / II VII$^{♯R}$ / VIIx$^{♯5}$ ♭VIIx / VI$^{♯♯7}$ VI$^{♯7}$ /

VI IV$^{♯♯R}$ / ♭III ♭VIx / II V / ♭VIx / IV$^{♯♯R}$ / ♭Vø IVx / III VI /

Vm Ix / IVm ♭VIIx / IIIø ♭IIIx / II ♭IIx / I II / III VI / ♭III ♭VIx /

II IVø / III VI / II ♭IIx / I^{+6} / I^{+6} //

SPRING IS HERE—by Lorenz Hart and Richard Rodgers

The author would like to acknowledge the harmonic innovations of Bill Evans in the above chart.

LESSON 16.

Key of B

The following is a bass line for "Just Friends." Transfer the melody to manuscript paper, transposing from G to B major.

pick-up

$\flat$V // IV / IV^{+6} / IVm / $\flat$VIIx / III / VI / $\flat$III / $\flat$VIx / II / V / I /

VI / IIx / IIx / II V / Vm $\flat$V / IV / IV^{+6} / IVm / $\flat$VIIx / III / VI /

$\flat$III / $\flat$VIx / II / V / VII IIIx / VI$^{\sharp 7}$ VI / IIx / II $\flat$IIx / I^{+6} / I^{+6} //

JUST FRIENDS—Words by Sam M. Lewis, Music by John Klenner
  © 1931 Metro-Goldwyn-Mayer Inc. © renewed 1959.
  All rights administered by Robbins Music Corp., a catalogue of CBS Songs, a Division of CBS Inc.
  International copyright secured. All rights reserved.
  Used by permission.

LESSON 17.

Key of D$\flat$

The following is a bass line for "Bewitched, Bothered and Bewildered." Transfer the melody to manuscript paper, transposing from C to D$\flat$.

pick-up*

$\flat$IIx // I $\sharp$Io / II $\sharp$IIo / III IIIx$^{\sharp 5}$ / IV IVo / II$^{\sharp\sharp\frac{R}{3}}$ $\flat$IIIo /

II $\flat$IIo / II / $\flat$IIx / I $\sharp$Io / II $\sharp$IIo / III IIIx$^{\sharp 5}$ /

IV IVo / II$^{\sharp\sharp\frac{R}{3}}$ $\flat$IIIo / II V Vm $\flat$V / IV IV^{+6} /

III $\flat$IIIx / II$^{\sharp\sharp 7}$ II$^{\sharp 7}$ / II $\flat$IIx / I $\flat$IIx / I VI / II III /

IV IVo / III $\flat$IIIo / II $\flat$IIx / I $\sharp$Io / II $\sharp$IIo /

III IIIx$^{\sharp 5}$ / IV IVo / II$^{\sharp\sharp\frac{R}{3}}$ $\flat$IIIo / II $\flat$IIx / I^{+6} / I^{+6} //

BEWITCHED, BOTHERED, AND BEWILDERED—by Richard Rodgers and Lorenz Hart
  © 1939 by Chappell & Co., Inc. © renewed.
  International copyright secured. All rights reserved.
  Used by permission.

*The pick-up chord covers the pick-up notes which sometimes occur in popular tunes.

LESSON 18.

Key of F#

The following is a base line for "Come Rain Or Come Shine." Transfer the melody to manuscript paper, transposing from F to F# major.

I IV / VIIm IIIx / VI$^{\#\#7}$ / VI$^{\#7}$ / VI IIx / II V / Vm Ix / Vm bV /

IVm bVIIx / Im IVx / IVm bIII / II V / bVϕ VIIx / IIIϕ VIx /

bVIx V bV IVx / IIIx bIIIx IIx bIIx / I IV / VIIm IIIx / VI$^{\#\#7}$ /

VI$^{\#7}$ VI / IIx / bII bV / VIIm / IIIx / VIx VII$^{\#5}_{b\;b7}$ / Io I$^{\#R}_{b\;b7}$ / IIx III$^{b\,b7}$ /

IVx $\#$IVϕ / VI IIx / IVx IIIx$^{\#3}$ / VIx / VIx //

COME RAIN OR COME SHINE—by Harold Arlen and Johnny Mercer

LESSON 19.

Key of Gb

The following is a bass line for "I Didn't Know What Time It Was." Gb is, of course, equivalent to F#; it is well, however, for the student to become familiar with both spellings. Transfer the melody to manuscript paper, transposing from G to Gb major.

VIIm IIIx / VI IIx / VIIm IIIx / VI IIx / II VII / VI IV$^{\#\#R}$ / IV III /

II Im / VIIm IIIx / VI IIx / VIIm IIIx / VI IIx / II VII / VI IV$^{\#\#R}$ /

IV III / II V / VII$^{\#R}$ I / VII IIIx / VII bVIIx / VI IIx / II V /

I VI$^{\#\#R}$ / VI IIx / II Im / VIIm IIIx / VI IIx / VIIm IIIx / VI IIx /

II VII / VI IV$^{\#\#R}$ / IV III / IVm bVIIx / III VI / II V$^{\#3}$ / I^{+6} / I^{+6} //

I DIDN'T KNOW WHAT TIME IT WAS—by Richard Rodgers and Lorenz Hart

LESSON 20.

12 Key Transposition

The following is a bass line for "I Only Have Eyes for You." Number the melody notes according to their position in the scale and explore the composition in twelve keys. The purpose of this study is to give the student a clear picture of the value of this system (Roman numerals) in transposing to any key.

pick-up

♯Io // II ♯IIx / II V / III ♭IIIx / II ♭IIx / I II^{+6} / III IVm /

III VIx / ♭III ♭VIx / II ♯IIx / II V / III ♭IIIx / II ♭IIx /

I II^{+6} / III ♭VIIx / VIx / III ♭IIIx / II / IIø ♭IIx / I II /

III VI / ♭Vø / IVm ♭VIIx / III VIx / ♭III ♭VIx / II ♯IIx / II V /

III ♭IIIx / II ♭IIx / I II^{+6} / III IVm / VIIm IIIx / IIIø ♭IIIx /

II / ♭IIx / I^{+6} / I^{+6} //

SECTION III

LESSON 21.

Inversions

An inversion is a rearrangement of the tones of a scale-tone chord to allow for more smoothly progressing bass lines.

Fig. 1 illustrates the inversions of the I chord in the key of C.

Fig. 1.

| I | 1st inversion | 2nd inversion | 3rd inversion |

An inversion breaks the series of thirds characteristic of all scale-tone chords. Each inversion contains a second (B to C in Fig. 1). The second is the characteristic interval of the inversion and is used to spell the chord.

The distance from each note of the second to the bottom note is used to identify the position. Thus, in Fig. 2, in the first inversion, the distances are as follows:

C down to E — sixth $\big\}$
B down to E — fifth $\big\}$ symbol—I_5^6

Fig. 2.   Fig. 3.

I_5^6 I_3^4

In Fig. 3, in the second inversion:

C down to G — fourth $\big\}$
B down to G — third $\big\}$ symbol—I_3^4

In Fig. 4, in the third inversion:

C down to B — second $\}$ symbol—I_2

Fig. 4.

I_2

NOTE: In Fig. 4, it is only possible to spell C down to B.

NOTE: The quality of the interval (major or minor) does not affect the spelling.

Fig. 5 illustrates the II chord in the key of C with its inversions.

Fig. 5.

II   II$^6_5$ II$^4_3$ II$_2$

Fig. 6 illustrates the III chord in the key of C with its inversions.

Fig. 6.

III   III$^6_5$ III$^4_3$ III$_2$

Fig. 7 illustrates the IV chord in the key of C with its inversions.

Fig 7.

IV   IV$^6_5$ IV$^4_3$ IV$_2$

Fig. 8 illustrates the V chord in the key of C with its inversions.

Fig. 8.

V   V$^6_5$ V$^4_3$ V$_2$

Fig. 9 illustrates the VI chord in the key of C with its inversions.

Fig. 9.

VI   VI$^6_5$ VI$^4_3$ VI$_2$

Fig. 10 illustrates the VII chord in the key of C with its inversions.

Fig. 10.

VII   VII$^6_5$ VII$^4_3$ VII$_2$

It is also possible to invert altered (Lesson 4), chromatic (Lesson 5) and altered-chromatic (Lesson 5) scale-tone chords.

Fig. 11 illustrates the 60 scale-tone chords with their inversions. Jazz is basically a "root position" music, but a facility with inversions can be invaluable in strengthening a jazz bass line.

Fig. 11.

37

Since the M, x, m and φ can be played in four positions, this gives us 192 chords. Adding the 12 diminished chords, this gives us a total of 204 chords — the complete harmonic system of jazz.

LESSON 22.

Inversions

The following is a bass line for "No Moon at All." It is written in D minor, which is the relative minor of F major. The symbols refer to F major. Transfer the melody to manuscript paper.

VI^{+6} / $IIIx^6_5$ / Vo / $VIIm^4_3$ / VII^4_3 / $♭Vφ_2$ $IIIx^{\#5}$ / VI^{+6} Ix /

IVx $IIIx$ / VI^{+6} / $IIIx^6_5$ / Vo / $VIIm^4_3$ / VII^4_3 / $♭Vφ_2$ $IIIx^{\#5}$ / VI^{+6} /

VI^{+6} / VIx / VIx / IIx / IIx / V / V / I IV / VII $♭VIIx$ / VI^{+6} /

$IIIx^6_5$ / Vo / $VIIm^4_3$ / VII^4_3 / $♭Vφ_2$ $IIIx^{\#5}$ / VI^{+6} / VI^{+6} //

NOTE: VI^{+6} is also $♭Vφ^6_5$, but the function of the chord is an adjusted VI chord rather than an inverted $♭Vφ$.

Inversions

Here is a bass line for "Liza." Transfer the melody to manuscript paper.

I V$^4_3$ / ♯IIo VIx$^4_3$ / IIφ$^6_5$ ♯IVo / Vm Ix / IV IV^{+6} / III ♭IIIx /
II ♭IIx / I^{+6} ♯I / I V$^4_3$ / ♯IIo VIx$^4_3$ / IIφ$^6_5$ ♯IVo / Vm Ix / IV IV^{+6} /
III ♭IIIx / II ♭IIx / I^{+6} ♭VIIx / VI^{+6} ♭Vφ / VII ♭VIIx / VI ♭VIo /
Vm ♭V / IV IV^{+6} / IIIφ ♭IIIx / II II$_2$ / ♭VIx V / I V$^4_3$ / ♯IIo VIx$^4_3$ /
IIφ$^6_5$ ♯IVo / Vm Ix / IV IV^{+6} / III ♭IIIx / II ♭IIx / I^{+6} //

NOTE: I^{+6} is also VI$^6_5$, but the function of the chord is usually an adjusted I chord rather than an inverted VI chord.

Inversions

The following is a bass line for "Waltz for Debbie." Transfer the melody to manuscript paper.

This tune presents a special problem in that the chord chart for the melody (called the "head chart") is not the same as the chord chart for improvising on the tune (called the "blowing chart"). This problem will be treated more extensively in Volume IV. For now, here are the two charts for "Waltz for Debbie." Note modulation to the key of A and the return to the key of F. The "head" chart appears in 3/4 time with a transition to 4/4 time in the final six measures of the tune; the "blowing" chart appears in 4/4 time with a transition to 3/4 time in the final four measures in preparation for a return to the "head" chart.

HEAD CHART: Key of F, 3/4 time

(F)$^3_4$ I$^6_5$ / VI / II / VIIx$^6_5$ / IIIx$_2$ / VIx$^6_5$ / IIx$_2$ / V$^6_5$ / Ix$_2$ / II$^4_3$ /

(F)$^3_4$ IIϕ$^4_3$ / V́ IV́ / III / VI͂Io ♭V́ϕ$^4_3$ VI͂x$^4_3$ / IV́ V́ VI͂ / VI͂I Ī IĪ /

(F)$^3_4$ I$^6_5$ / VI / II / V / IIIx$^6_5$ / VIx$_2$ / IIx$^6_5$ / V$_2$ / IIIx$^{♯5}$ / V́I VI͂$_2$ //

(A)$^3_4$ II / V́ V́$_2$ / III / II / I / I$_2$ // (F)$^3_4$ II / V / III / VIx / II /

(F)$^3_4$ IIIx$^{♯5}$ / VI / Vm / IV / IIIx / VI / IIx / ♭IIIM / ♭VIM / II /

(F)$^3_4$ V / I$^6_5$ / VI / II / VIIx$^6_5$ / IIIx$_2$ / VIx$^6_5$ / IIx$_2$ / V$^6_5$ / Ix$_2$ / II$^4_3$ /

(F)$^3_4$ IIϕ$^4_3$ / VI͂$_2$ V́$_2$ / III / VIx / ♭Vm / VIIx$^6_5$ / I͂$^6_5$ V́$^4_3$ / Ix / IV /

(F)$^3_4$ IIIx$^{♯5}$ / VI / ♭VIx / VI$_2$ / VM$^{♯3}_{♯5}$ / V$^{♯3}$ / V$^{♭5}$ // (F)$^4_4$ VI$_2$ VM$^{♯3}_{♯5}$ /

(F)$^4_4$ V$^{♯3}$ V$^{♭5}$ / VI$_2$ VM$^{♯3}_{♯5}$ / V$^{♯3}$ V$^{♭5}$ / I^{+6} / I^{+6} //

BLOWING CHART: Key of F, 4/4 time

(F)$^4_4$ III VI / II V / IIIx VIx / IIx V / Ix IV^{+6} / IIϕ V / III VI /

(F)$^4_4$ II V / III VI / II V / IIIx VIx / IIx V / IIIx VI // (A)$^4_4$ II V / I /

(A)$^4_4$ I // (F)$^4_4$ II V / III VIx / II IIIx / VI Vm / IV IIIx / VI IIx /

(F)$^4_4$ ♭IIIm ♭VIM / II V / III VI / II V / IIIx VI / IIx V / Ix IV^{+6} /

(F)$^4_4$ IIϕ V / III VIx / ♭Vm VIIx / III Ix / IV IIIx / VI / IIx ♭Vo /

(F)$^4_4$ III ♭IIIo / II V // (F)$^3_4$ I^{+6} / ♭IIIo / II / V //

Da Capo to head.

WALTZ FOR DEBBY—by Bill Evans and Gene Lees
TRO © 1964 and 1965 Acorn Music Corp., New York, N.Y.
U.K. © 1962 Acorn Music Inc. Assigned to Kensington Music Ltd., 85 Gower Street,
London, WC1 for the territory of the world excluding USA and Canada
Used by permission.

Inversions

The following is a bass line for "Giant Steps." Unlike the bass lines in this volume, the chords are indicated by letters instead of the usual Roman numerals. The reason for this is that "Giant Steps" has no prevailing key center but, instead, a series of implied key centers.

BM Dx$^{4}_{3}$ / GM B♭x$^{4}_{3}$ / E♭M / Am Dx / GM B♭x$^{4}_{3}$ / E♭M F♯x$^{4}_{3}$ /

BM / Fm B♭x / E♭M / Am Dx / GM / C♯m F♯x / BM / Fm B♭x /

E♭M / C♯m F♯x / BM Dx$^{4}_{3}$ / GM B♭x$^{4}_{3}$ / E♭M / Am Dx / GM B♭$^{4}_{3}$ /

E♭M F♯x$^{4}_{3}$ / BM / Fm B♭x / E♭M / Am Dx / GM / C♯m F♯x /

BM / Fm B♭x / E♭M / E♭M //

GIANT STEPS—by John Coltrane
© 1974 Jowcol Music
Used by permission.

The symbol key for the preceding chord chart is as follows:

M—major
x—dominant
m—minor

SECTION IV

LESSON 26.

Modulation

Many of the popular tunes used as jazz material modulate from one key to another in the course of a 32-bar chorus. This modulation is seldom indicated in sheet music although the jazz musician "thinks" in these key changes for simplicity and order. The following six lessons will deal with tunes of this type. A simple rule for identifying the presence of a new key is the appearance of a major chord on other than I or IV (i.e., IIIM, ♭VIM, etc.).

The following is a bass line for "Body and Soul" in D♭. The original key of this tune is C major, but since 1930, the year the tune was written, convention has prevailed in favor of D♭. Transfer the melody to manuscript paper using the following signatures: bars 1 - 15, key of D♭; bar 16, beats 1, 2, key of D♭; bar 16, beats 3, 4, key of D; bars 17 - 20, key of D; bars 21 - 23, key of C; bar 24, beats 1, 2, key of C; bar 24, beats 3, 4, key of D♭; bars 25 - 32, key of D♭. The letters in parentheses indicate the key in which the symbols are to be played.

(D♭) II$^{\sharp\sharp7}$ II$^{\sharp7}$ / II ♭IIx / I II / III ♭IIIo / II II$_2$ / VII ♭VIIx /

(D♭) V̄Ī IĪ ♭IĪx / I ♯Io / II$^{\sharp\sharp7}$ II$^{\sharp7}$ / II ♭IIx / I II / III ♭IIIo /

(D♭) II II$_2$ / VII ♭VIIx / V̄Ī IĪ ♭IĪx / I^{+6}　　(D) V / I^{+6} II /

(D) VI$^{4}_{3}$ IVm / IĪI V̄Ī IĪ IV̄o / III ♭IIIx II ♭IIx // (C) II V /

(C) I ♭IIIo / II ♭IIX / Īx VĪIx　　(D♭) V̄Ix / II$^{\sharp\sharp7}$ II$^{\sharp7}$ / II ♭IIx /

(D♭) I II / III ♭IIIo / II II$_2$ / VII ♭VIIx / V̄Ī IĪ ♭IĪx / I^{+6} //

BODY AND SOUL—Lyrics by Edward Heyman, Robert Sour, and Frank Eyton, Music by John Green
© 1930 (renewed) Warner Bros. Inc. All rights reserved.
Used by permission.

LESSON 27.

Modulation

The following is a bass line for "How High the Moon," in the key of G. Transfer the melody to manuscript paper following the signatures indicated by the letters.

pick-up
(G) V$^{\sharp 3}$ // I / I^{+6} / (F) II / ♭IIx / I / I^{+6} / (E♭) II / ♭IIx /

(E♭) I VI / ♭Vφ VIIx / III^{+6} / (G) V$^{\sharp 3}$ / I II / III IV$^{♭3}$ /

(G) III ♭IIIx / II V$^{\sharp 3}$ / I / I^{+6} / (F) II / ♭IIx / I / I^{+6} / (E♭) II /

(E♭) ♭IIx / I VI / (G) IIφ V / I II / III IV$^{♭3}$ / III ♭IIIx /

(G)   II ♭IIx / I^{+6} / I^{+6} //

LESSON 28.

Modulation

The following is a bass line for "Laura," in the key of C. Transfer the melody to manuscript paper following the signatures indicated by the letters.

(G) II / ♭IIx / I / I^{+6} / (F) II / ♭IIx / I / I^{+6} / (E♭) II /

(E♭) ♭IIx / I / VI / (G) IIφ V$^{♭5}$ / V$^{♭5}$ IVo / III / ♭IIIx / II /

(G) ♭IIx / I / I^{+6} / (F) II / ♭IIx / I / I^{+6} / (C) IVm / IVo / III /

(C) VI / IIx$^{♭5}$ / II V$^{\sharp 3}$ / I^{+6} / I^{+6} //

As indicated above, "Laura," in the key of C, does not start in the key of C. However, the tune comes to a final close in the key of C which definitely establishes the key.

LESSON 29.

Modulation

The following is a bass line for "I'll Remember April," in the key of G. Transfer the melody to manuscript paper following the signatures indicated by the letters.

(G) I / I / IVx / I / Im / Im$_2$ / VIϕ / IIx / II / V /
(G) IIIϕ / ♭IIIx / II / ♭IIx / I / I^{+6} / (B♭) II / V / I IVo /
(B♭) III ♭IIIx / II / V / I / I^{+6} / (G) II / V / I / IV /
(E) II / ♭IIx / I VI / (G) II ♭IIx / I / I / IVx / I / Im /
(G) Im$_2$ / VIϕ / IIx / II / V / IIIϕ / ♭IIIx / II / ♭IIx /
(G) I^{+6} / I^{+6} //

I'LL REMEMBER APRIL—Words and Music by Don Raye, Gene De Paul, and Pat Johnston
© 1941, 1942 by MCA Music, a Division of MCA Inc., New York, N.Y. © renewed and assigned to MCA Music, a Division of MCA Inc. and PIC Corp., New York, N.Y. All rights reserved.
Used by permission.

LESSON 30.

Modulation

The following is a bass line for "All the Things You Are," in the key of A♭. Transfer the melody to manuscript paper following the signatures indicated by the letters.

(A♭) VI / II / V / I / IV / (C) V / I / I^{+6} /
(E♭) VI / II / V / I / IV / (G) V / I / VI / II /
(G) V$^{\#3}$ / I / I^{+6} / (E) II / ♭IIx / I / I^{+6} /
(A♭) VI / II / V / I / IV / IVm / III / ♭IIIo / II /
(A♭) V$^{\#3}$ ♭IIx / I^{+6} / I^{+6} //

ALL THE THINGS YOU ARE—by Jerome Kern and Oscar Hammerstein II
© 1939 T.B. Harms Co. © renewed % The Welk Music Group.
International copyright secured. All rights reserved.
Used by permission.

LESSON 31.

Modulation

The following is a bass line for "Autumn in New York," in F. Transfer the melody to manuscript paper following the signatures indicated by the letters.

(F) II III / IV V$^{\#3}$ / I^{+6} I / I II III ♭III / II III /
(F) IV V / III VIx / IIIϕ ♭IIIx / II III / (A♭) II ♭IIx /
(A♭) I II / (E♭) VI VII / I$^{\#5}$ ♭Vϕ / (C) II ♭IIx / I VII /
(F) III ♭III / II III / IV V$^{\#3}$ / I^{+6} I / I II III IV /
(F) Vm VI / (D♭) II IIIx$^{\#5}$ / VI VI$_2$ / ♭Vϕ IVx / III^{+6}VIIx$^{\#5}$ /
(D♭) III ♭III II ♭IIx / I ♭IIx / I VII VI Vm / (F) II III /
(F) IVm V$^{\#5}$ / Im^{+6} / Im^{+6} //

AUTUMN IN NEW YORK—Words and music by Vernon Duke
© 1934 (renewed) Warner Bros. Inc.
All rights reserved.
Used by permission.

LESSON 32.

Transposition—Modulation

Fig. 1 is a lead sheet of "In Your Own Sweet Way" by Dave Brubeck. Fig. 1 represents the composer's view of his composition; Fig. 2 represents a figured bass solution of the same tune.

Fig. 1. "In Your Own Sweet Way."

47

Both Fig. 1 and Fig. 2 present the essential "facts" of the composition; Fig. 1 represents the composer's original conception of the piece, and Fig. 2 represents the author's view of the essential structure of the tune seen through twenty-five years of social usage.

Note the appearance in Fig. 2 of key changes which social consensus has established as part of the fabric of the tune.

The key series for transposition will be:
I—bVI—I—bVI—I—III—II—I—bVI—I.

The following is a bass line for "In Your Own Sweet Way" in Bb. The key order is as follows:
Bb—Gb—Bb—Gb—Bb—D—C—Bb—Gb—Bb.

In Roman numerals this reads:
I—bVI—I—bVI—I—III—II—I—bVI—I as above.

Fig. 2. "In Your Own Sweet Way."

pick-up
(Bb) IV // VIIm IIIx / VI IIx / II V / I IV // (Gb) II V / I IV //

(Bb) IIϕ bIIx / I IV / VIIm IIIx / VI IIx / II V / I IV //

(Gb) II V / I IV // (Bb) IIϕ bIIx / I VI // (D) II V / I VI /

(D) II V / I // (C) II V / I VIx^{b5} // (Bb) IVm bVIIx / VIx ♯VIo /

(Bb) VIIm IIIx / VI IIx / II V / I IV // (Gb) II V / I IV //

(Bb) IIϕ bIIx / I //

IN YOUR OWN SWEET WAY—by Dave Brubeck
    © 1955 Derry Music Co.
    Used by permission.

When transposing this tune, number the melody tones according to the prevailing key in the bass line. Transpose to various keys as a transposition problem.

SECTION V

LESSON 33.

Arpeggios

The basic problem of jazz improvisation is to abandon the melody and build an improvised line on the elements of the chords in a tune. Thus, we will combine the vertical (left hand) with the horizontal (right hand). The chord elements are as follows: (1) Arpeggios; (2) Scales; (3) Chromatic tones. Thus, jazz improvisation employs a twelve-tone line (twelve chromatic tones in the octave) superimposed on the sixty chord system.

An arpeggio is a "broken" chord moving in alternate steps. The following illustrates the arpeggios of the five qualities on C for two octaves.

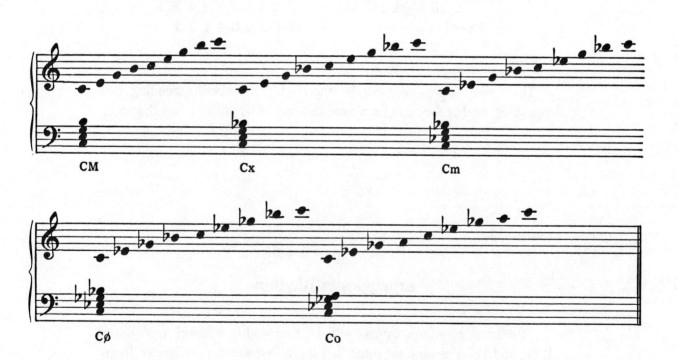

These notes should be played ascending and descending.

Using the chord chart on pages 25 and 26, practice the arpeggios for the sixty scale-tone chords using the following fingering.

C — 5 qualities	1 2 3 4 1 2 3 4 5
D — 5 qualities	1 2 3 4 1 2 3 4 5
E — 5 qualities	1 2 3 4 1 2 3 4 5
F — 5 qualities	1 2 3 4 1 2 3 4 5
G — 5 qualities	1 2 3 4 1 2 3 4 5
A — 5 qualities	1 2 3 4 1 2 3 4 5
B — 5 qualities	1 2 3 4 1 2 3 4 5
D♭ — 5 qualities	2 1 2 3 4 1 2 3 4
A♭ — 5 qualities	2 1 2 3 4 1 2 3 4
B♭ M — x	2 1 2 3 4 1 2 3 4
B♭ — A♯ m — ø — o	2 3 1 2 3 4 1 2 3
G♭ M — x	2 3 4 1 2 3 4 1 2
G♭ — F♯ m — ø — o	2 1 2 3 4 1 2 3 4
E♭ M — x	2 1 2 3 4 1 2 3 4
E♭ m (the only arpeggio with all black notes)	1 2 3 4 1 2 3 4 5
E♭ — D♯ ø — o	2 3 1 2 3 4 1 2 3

These sixty arpeggios must be thoroughly mastered, ascending and descending, so that they can be played automatically with correct fingering.

LESSON 34.

Arpeggios in Rhythm

Rhythmic problems in jazz will be thoroughly studied in Volumes II, III and IV. The student must first learn "what" to play before learning "how" to play it. For now, the following basic material on rhythm will suffice.

The rhythmic division of the front and rear lines of a 1900 New Orleans jazz band was as follows:

Eighth–note (♪) — trumpet
Whole–note (𝅝) or half note (𝅗𝅥) — tuba or trombone
Quarter–note (♩) — drums
Technically this is a form of florid counterpoint involving three kinds of time played simultaneously. This is the essence of the jazz beat.

This rhythmic counterpoint is always present in jazz, although these three levels of time can be assigned to various instruments. In a modern group, the rhythmic breakdown is as follows:

Eighth–note (♪)   —   trumpet
Whole note (𝅝) or half–note (𝅗𝅥)   —   piano
Quarter–note (♩)   —   bass

Transferred to the keyboard, the rhythmic assignment is as follows:

Eighth–note (♪)   —   right hand
Whole note (𝅝) or half–note (𝅗𝅥)   —   left hand
Quarter–note (♩)   —   foot beat

This rhythmic composite is occasionally interrupted, but its continuing presence is essential to jazz improvisation.

As soon as the student has become familiar with the chords of a tune, a quarter-note beat should be tapped by the foot in order to create the basis for a jazz beat.

In succeeding chapters, we will explore the three fundamental rhythmic structures used in jazz improvisation — the eighth–note, the eighth–note triplet and the sixteenth–note. The jazz line can employ rhythmic values up to the thirty-second–note. See Fig. 1. However, for practical purposes we will limit our work to the three above-named values.

Fig. 1.

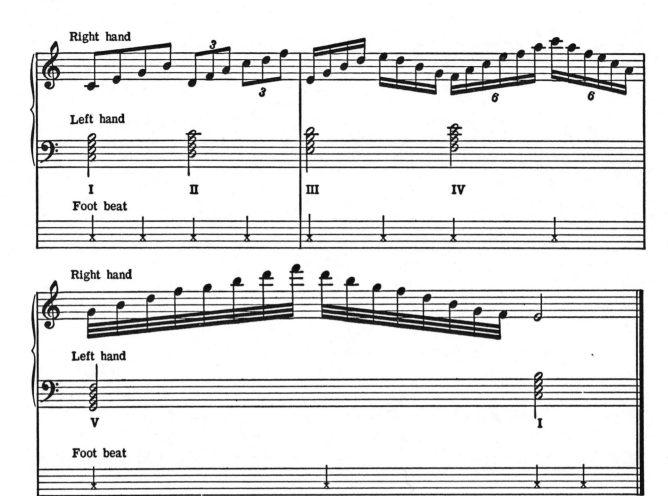

I chord   —   eighth notes
II chord   —   eighth-note triplets
III chord   —   sixteenth notes
IV chord   —   sixteenth-note triplets
V chord   —   thirty-second notes

Rest values of both more and less than an eighth note are equally important in the jazz line.

A dot adds half the value to either a note or a rest.

In Fig.2:

I and II chord — whole-note rest (four beats)
III chord — half-note rest (two beats)
V chord — dotted quarter-note rest
♭Vø chord — quarter-note rest
IVm chord — dotted eighth-note rest
III chord — eighth-note rest
♭III chord — dotted sixteenth-note rest
II chord — sixteenth-note rest

52

Fig. 2.

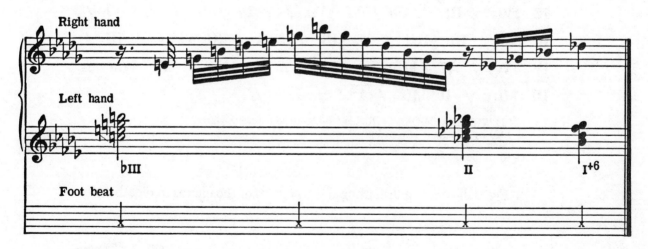

LESSON 35.

Eighth-note Arpeggios

Fig. 1 is a bass line for "I Could Write a Book," in the key of D♭. The sheet music appears in the key of C, so the melody must be transposed. Transfer the melody to manuscript paper using three staves — one for melody, one for an improvised line and the third for the chord symbols. As a starting point for improvisation, abandon the melody and play the arpeggios of the chords in eighth notes. Try to keep an uninterrupted quarter-note beat with the foot — no pedal.

Do not "set" the improvised figures. Use the arpeggios both ascending and descending as well as from the various inversion points (third, fifth and seventh). Respect the fingering shown on page 50 at all times.

The following rules will be helpful in fingering problems:

1. All inversion arpeggios beginning on a white note begin with the thumb.

2. All inversion arpeggios beginning on a black note begin with the index finger (except E♭ minor which begins with the thumb) and go to the thumb on the first white note.

Fig. 1.

pick-up
♭IIx // I VI / II IVo / III ♭IIIx / II ♭IIx / I II /

III VI / II III / IV IVo / VI⁴₃ ♭IIIo / II V / ♭Vφ IVx /

III ♯VIo / III⁴₃ ♭VIIo / VI ♭VIx / V IV / III II / I VI /

II IVo / III ♭IIIx / II ♭IIx / I II / III VI / II III /

IV IVo / VI⁴₃ ♭IIIo / II V / Vm ♭V / IV IVm /

III ♭IIIx / II ♭IIx / I⁺⁶ / I⁺⁶ //

Fig. 2 illustrates a drill using the arpeggios of the chords in eighth notes.

Fig. 2.

DRILL: Study Fig. 2 and explore various eighth-note arpeggio lines on the chords of Fig. 1. In the beginning, the student may write out a line as a starting point.

LESSON 36.

Rhythmic Combinations—On Green Dolphin Street

Fig. 1 is a bass line for "Green Dolphin Street" in E♭. Transfer the melody to manuscript paper using three staves as in the previous lesson. Note the modulation to G♭ major and the return to E♭.

(E♭) I^{+6} / I / Im / Im / IIx$_2$ / ♭IIM$_2$ / I / ♯Io / II / ♭IIx / I / VI //

(G♭) II / ♭IIx / I ♯IV // (E♭) II ♭IIx / I^{+6} / I / Im / Im / IIx$_2$ /

(E♭) ♭IIM$_2$ / I / ♯Io / II II$_2$ / VII ♭VIIx / VI VI$_2$ / ♭V∅ IVx /

(E♭) III ♭IIIx / II ♭IIx / I / I^{+6} //

Fig. 2 illustrates a drill using the arpeggios of the chords in eighth-note triplets.

61

DRILL: Study Fig. 2 and explore the various eighth-note triplet arpeggio
lines on the chords of Fig. 1. Write out the lines if necessary.

Sixteenth-note Arpeggios

Now that we have investigated a line employing the eighth note (two notes to a foot beat) and the eighth-note triplet (three notes to a foot beat), we will explore, in this chapter, the sixteenth-note line (four notes to a foot beat).

Fig. 1 is a bass line for "At Long Last Love," in C. Transfer the melody to manuscript paper using three staves.

Fig. 1.

$\overset{\text{pick-up}}{\flat\text{IIx}}$ // I^{+6} / VII / VI / III$^{6}_{5}$ / IV / III $\flat$IIIx / II / II$_2$ /

VII$^{6}_{5}$ / $\flat$IIϕ / II$_2$ / VII / II$^{4}_{3}$ / V$^{\sharp 3}$ / I^{+6} / $\flat$IIx / I^{+6} /

VII / VI / III$^{6}_{5}$ / Ix Vm$^{4}_{3}$ / $\sharp$IIo IIIϕ / IV^{+6} / IV /

$\flat$Vϕ / IIϕ^{6}_{5} / III / $\flat$IIIx / II / $\flat$IIx / I^{+6} / I^{+6} //

Fig. 2 illustrates a sixteenth-note drill employing the arpeggios of the chords in Fig. 1.

Fig. 2.

65

DRILL: Write out or play a sixteenth-note arpeggio line on Fig. 1.

LESSON 38.

Rhythmic Combinations

Since the problem of shifting from one rhythm to another is of the utmost importance in playing a jazz line, we will now consider combining the rhythms in Lessons 35, 36 and 37. Under no circumstances can the shift from one rhythm to another be allowed to disturb the quarter-note foot beat.

Fig. 1 is a bass line for "Sophisticated Lady," in A♭. Transfer the melody to manuscript paper using three staves. Note key changes.

Fig. 1.

(A♭)   II#♯♭7   II♯7   II / ♭VIIx VIx ♭VIx V / I IVx /

(A♭)   Ix VIIx ♭VIIx VIx / IIx / II ♭IIx / I / ♯Io /

(A♭)   II♯♯7   II♯7   II / ♭VIIx VIx ♭VIx V / I IVx /

(A♭)   Ix VIIx ♭VIIx VIx / IIx / II ♭IIx / I +6 / (G) IIø ♭IIx /

(G)   I VI / II V / III ♭IIIx / II ♭IIx / I VI / II V /

(G)   I ♭V (A♭) III / II VII IIIø ♭IIIx / II♯♯7 II♯7 II /

(A♭)   ♭VIIx VIx ♭VIx V / I IVx / Ix VIIx ♭VIIx VIx /

(A♭)   IIx / II ♭IIx / I +6 / I +6 //

Fig. 2 illustrates a drill employing eighth note, eighth-note triplets and sixteenth-note rhythms in various combinations.

Fig. 2.

DRILL: Write or play a line on the chords of Fig. 1 using eighth note, eighth-note triplets and sixteenth note rhythms. Keep an uninterrupted quarter-note foot beat when playing.

70

Rhythmic Composites (ballad)

Now that we have some facility with abandoning the melody and using the arpeggios of the chords, we may consider combining the note and rest values studied in Lesson 34 into four-bar composites which allow us to shift suddenly from one rhythm to another or introduce a rest value without disturbing the foot beat. Fig. 1 is a possible four-bar composite for a slow tune:

Fig. 1.

This composite reads as follows:
    The first line will apply to the first bar of a tune;
    The second line to the second bar;
    The third line to the third bar;
    The fourth line to the fourth bar.

Then we start over again:
    The first line to the fifth bar;
    The second line to the sixth bar; and so on until the end of the tune.

Fig. 2 is a bass line for "I Got It Bad," in G.

Fig. 2.

I II / III VI / IIx VI$^{4}_{3}$ / IVo ♯IVϕ / II II$_2$ / ♭VĨIx VĨx ♭VĨx V̂ /

I^{+6} ♯Io / II ♭IIx / I II / III VI / IIx VI$^{4}_{3}$ / IVo ♯IVϕ / II II$_2$ /

♭VĨIx VĨx ♭VĨx V̄ / Ī$^{∓6}$ VĨ ♭VĨ / Vm ♭V / IV^{+6} / IV^{+6} / IVm^{+6} /

♭VIIx / I IV / III ♭IIIx / II / V$^{♯3}$ / I II / III VI / IIx VI$^{4}_{3}$ /

IVo ♯IVϕ / II II$_2$ / ♭VĨIx VĨx ♭VĨx V̄ / I^{+6} / I^{+6} //

I GOT IT BAD AND THAT AIN'T GOOD—by Paul Francis Webster and
Duke Ellington

If we apply our composite to the arpeggios of Fig. 2, we derive the
following drill.

DRILL: Transfer the melody to manuscript paper using three staves: one for melody; one for the student's improvisation; one for the bass line. Using Fig. 3 as a model, the student should write out, if necessary, an improvisation using the composite and the arpeggios of the bass line in Fig. 2.

LESSON 40.

Rhythmic Composite (up-tempo)

In the quicker tempos in jazz, the composite usually becomes more simple in order to avoid a cluttered sound and to insure a strong pulse.

The following is a possible up-tempo composite:

Fig. 1 is a bass line for "You Took Advantage of Me," in E♭.

Fig. 1.

I ♯Io / II V / III ♭IIIo / II V / Vm Ix / IV ♭VIIx / IIIx VIx IIx V /

I⁺⁶ ♯I / I ♯Io / II V / III ♭IIIo / II V / Vm Ix / IV ♭VIIx /

IIIx VIx IIx V / I⁺⁶ ♭VIIx / V̂Î⁺⁶ ♭V̂ϕ VÎIx / IIIx VIx / IIx V /

I ♭VIIx / V̂Î⁺⁶ ♭V̂ϕ VÎIx / IIIx VIx / IIx V / III ♭IIIx II ♭IIx /

I ♯Io / II V / III ♭IIIo / II V / Vm Ix / IV ♭VIIx / IIIx VIx IIx V /

I⁺⁶ //

Fig. 2.   If we apply the composite to the arpeggios of Fig. 1, we derive the following drill.

As in Lesson 39, the student should thoroughly analyze the use of rest values and arpeggios in Fig. 2. Simply to play over these specimens is of little value. When playing these examples, try to keep a steady quarter-note foot beat. Above all, do not use any pedal.

DRILL: Transfer the melody to manuscript paper using three staves: one for melody; one for the student's improvisation; and one for the bass line. Using Fig. 2 as a model, the student should write out, if necessary, an improvisation on the bass line in Fig. 1.

SECTION VI

LESSON 41.

Modes

If we play the scale-tone chords in C and play the C major scale from root to root of each chord (Fig. 1), we are playing the various modes of the scale of C. *A mode is a displaced scale played from root to root of the chord.*

Fig. 1.

CHORD	SCALE	DISPLACEMENT	MODE
I	C	C - C	IONIAN
II	C	D - D	DORIAN
III	C	E - E	PHRYGIAN
IV	C	F - F	LYDIAN
V	C	G - G	MIXOLYDIAN
VI	C	A - A	AEOLIAN
VII	C	B - B	LOCRIAN

Fig. 2 illustrates the modes of the scale of G:

CHORD	SCALE	DISPLACEMENT	MODE
I	G	G - G	IONIAN
II	G	A - A	DORIAN
III	G	B - B	PHRYGIAN
IV	G	C - C	LYDIAN
V	G	D - D	MIXOLYDIAN
VI	G	E - E	AEOLIAN
VII	G	F♯ - F♯	LOCRIAN

The following table illustrates the modes existing in any key:

CHORD	DISPLACEMENT	MODE
I	1 - 1	IONIAN
II	2 - 2	DORIAN
III	3 - 3	PHRYGIAN
IV	4 - 4	LYDIAN
V	5 - 5	MIXOLYDIAN
VI	6 - 6	AEOLIAN
VII	7 - 7	LOCRIAN

These modes built on the twelve major scales represent one of the most important elements of jazz improvisation. They are highly effective in building a horizontal "blowing" line so long as the harmonic line moves in the normal scale-tone chords without alteration or chromatic adjustment. Since the previous lessons have made it evident that even the simplest tune utilizes altered and chromatic chords, this simple modal system must be expanded to meet the requirements of a sixty chord system. The next six lessons will deal with this problem. In preparation for these chapters, the student is strongly advised to play the scale-tone chords in twelve keys with accompanying modes in the right hand as in Figs. 3 and 4.

Fig. 3. Key of C.

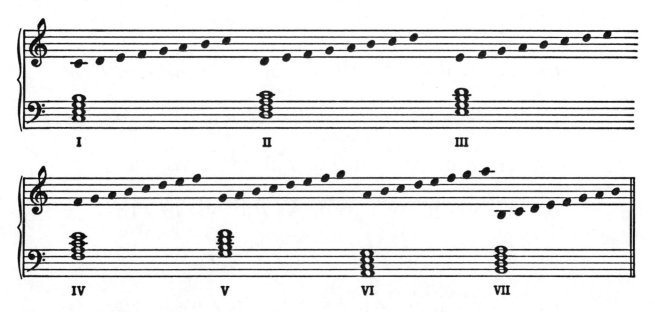

Fig. 4. Key of G.

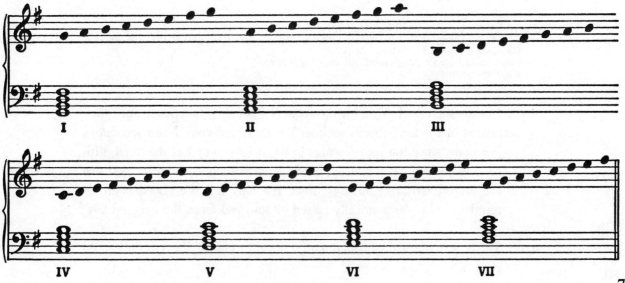

Fig. 5 is a bass line for "Speak Low," in F. Transfer the melody to manuscript paper noting key changes. On the lettered scale-tone chords, abandon the melody and play the required mode of the prevailing key scale. Letters over each chord indicate the mode to be played with each chord.

The following chart illustrates the symbol key for each mode:

Ionian — IO	Mixolydian — M
Dorian — D	Aeolian — A
Phrygian — P	Locrian — LO
Lydian — LY	

Fig. 5.

pick-up

(F)   #Io   // $\overset{\text{D of F}}{\text{II}}$ / $\overset{\text{M of F}}{\text{V}}$ / $\overset{\text{D of F}}{\text{II}}$ / $\overset{\text{M of F}}{\text{V}}$ / $\overset{\text{D of F}}{\text{II}}$ / $\overset{\text{M of F}}{\text{V}}$ / $\overset{\text{see note}}{\text{Vm}}$ / Ix //

(Ab) $\overset{\text{D of Ab}}{\text{II}}$ / $\overset{\text{M of Ab}}{\text{V}}$ / $\overset{\text{D of Ab}}{\text{II}}$ / $\overset{\text{M of Ab}}{\text{V}}$ // (F) $\overset{\text{P of F}}{\text{III}}$ $\overset{\text{A of F}}{\text{VI}}$ / $\overset{\text{D of F}}{\text{II}}$ $\overset{\text{M of F}}{\text{V}}$ / $\overset{\text{Io of F}}{\text{I}^{+6}}$ /

(F)   #Io   / $\overset{\text{D of F}}{\text{II}}$ / $\overset{\text{M of F}}{\text{V}}$ / $\overset{\text{D of F}}{\text{II}}$ / $\overset{\text{M of F}}{\text{V}}$ / $\overset{\text{D of F}}{\text{II}}$ / $\overset{\text{M of F}}{\text{V}}$ / Vm / Ix //

(Ab) $\overset{\text{D of Ab}}{\text{II}}$ / $\overset{\text{M of Ab}}{\text{V}}$ / $\overset{\text{D of Ab}}{\text{II}}$ / $\overset{\text{M of Ab}}{\text{V}}$ // (F) $\overset{\text{P of F}}{\text{III}}$ $\overset{\text{A of F}}{\text{VI}}$ / $\overset{\text{D of F}}{\text{II}}$ $\overset{\text{M of F}}{\text{V}}$ / $\overset{\text{Io of F}}{\text{I}^{+6}}$ / $\overset{\text{Io of F}}{\text{I}^{+6}}$ //

(Eb) $\overset{\text{D of Eb}}{\text{II}}$ / $\overset{\text{D of Eb}}{\text{II}}$ / $\overset{\text{see note}}{\flat\text{VIIx}}$ / $\flat$VIIx / $\overset{\text{Io of Eb}}{\text{I}}$ / $\overset{\text{Io of Eb}}{\text{I}}$ // (F) $\overset{\text{see note}}{\flat\text{VIx}}$ / $\overset{\text{M of F}}{\text{V}}$ /

(F) $\overset{\text{D of F}}{\text{II}}$ / $\overset{\text{M of F}}{\text{V}}$ / $\overset{\text{D of F}}{\text{II}}$ / $\overset{\text{M of F}}{\text{V}}$ / $\overset{\text{D of F}}{\text{II}}$ / $\overset{\text{M of F}}{\text{V}}$ / Vm / Ix / IVm / $\flat$VIIx /

(F) $\overset{\text{P of F}}{\text{III}}$ / $\overset{\text{A of F}}{\text{VI}}$ / $\overset{\text{D of F}}{\text{II}}$ / $\overset{\text{see note}}{\text{V}^{\#7}_{\#5}}$ / $\overset{\text{Io of F}}{\text{I}^{+6}}$ / $\overset{\text{Io of F}}{\text{I}^{+6}}$ //

NOTE: Chords such as **II**, **V** or **I** are considered *primary functions*, since they belong to the key; chords such as **Vm** or **Ix** are considered *secondary functions*, since the root remains in the original key but the third, fifth or seventh have been altered; finally, chords such as $\flat$**VIIx** or $\flat$**VIx** are considered *tertiary functions*, since not only has the chord been altered but also chromatically raised or lowered from the original key.

NOTE: $V^{\#7}_{\#5}$ is actually a major-augmented seventh chord; the symbol would read V^{M}_{+}.

The Major Scale

The major chord in any key appears on I and IV.

CHORD	DISPLACEMENT	MODE
I	1 - 1	Ionian
IV	4 - 4	Lydian

In determining which of these two modes to choose, the deciding factor must be the relative strength of these two major positions in diatonic harmony. On the basis of this, there can be no doubt of the overwhelming feeling of I when hearing a major chord. For this reason, the major chord takes the Ionian mode (1 - 1) except in cases where the bass line gives a strong feeling of IV, e.g. I II / III IV / V I / (*see* Fig. 1).

Fig. 1.

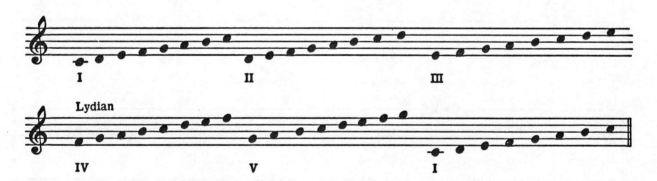

Here the use of the Ionian mode of the scale of F on the IV chord would destroy the feeling of C major running through the entire bass line and the Lydian mode (4 - 4) should be used. Except in cases of this sort, the Ionian mode is employed on all major chords.

Fig. 2 illustrates the twelve major chords with accompanying Ionian modes, to be played both ascending and descending.

Fig. 2.

RULE: *The major chord is a I or the temporary I of a new key and takes the scale of that key from root to root.*

Fig. 3 is a bass line for "Moonlight in Vermont." Transfer the melody to manuscript paper following the key signatures indicated by the letters. Abandon the melody and play the appropriate mode on each major chord. Major^{+6} chords follow the same rule as normal major chords.

Fig. 3.

(E♭) I⁺⁶ VI / II ♭IIx / I⁺⁶ VI / ♭VIIx / II V♯³ /
(E♭) I⁺⁶ ♯I / I⁺⁶ VI / II ♭IIx / I⁺⁶ VI / ♭VIIx /
(E♭) II V♯³ / I⁺⁶ / (G) II IVo / III ♭IIIx / II ♭IIx / I /
(A♭) II IVo / III ♭IIIx / II ♭IIx / I ♭VIx /
(E♭) I⁺⁶ VI / II ♭IIx / I⁺⁶ VI / ♭VIIx / II V♯³ /
(E♭) I⁺⁶ VI / ♭Vφ IIx ♭IIx / I //

MOONLIGHT IN VERMONT—by John Blackburn and Karl Suessdorf
© 1944–1945 Michael H. Goldsen, Inc. © renewed 1972.
Used by permission.

LESSON 43.

The Dominant Scale

The dominant chord in any key appears on V only.

CHORD	DISPLACEMENT	MODE
V	5 - 5	Mixolydian

Since the dominant chord only occurs at the position of V, there can be no doubt concerning the accompanying mode. The dominant always takes the Mixolydian mode.

Dominant chords on other than V (IIIx, ♭VIx, etc.) are considered a temporary V of some other key. Thus, in the key of C:

CHORD	SPELLING	SCALE OR KEY	DISPLACEMENT
Ix	Temporary V	F	C - C
IIx	Temporary V	G	D - D
IIIx	Temporary V	A	E - E
IVx	Temporary V	B♭	F - F
V	Natural V	C	G - G
VIx	Temporary V	D	A - A
VIIx	Temporary V	E	B - B
♭IIx	Temporary V	G♭	D♭ - D♭

In jazz harmony, these temporary dominants seldom resolve to their natural majors [i.e., in the key of C—III ♭IIIx II ♭IIx I is a normal pattern; the ♭IIIx (E♭x) does not go to A♭M, the ♭IIx (D♭x) does not go to G♭M]. However, at the moment they are played, they imply the V of a new key.

83

Fig. 1 illustrates the twelve dominant chords with accompanying
Mixolydian modes, to be played both ascending and descending.

Fig. 1.

RULE: *The dominant chord is a V or the temporary V of a new key and
takes the scale of that key from root to root.*

Fig. 2 is a bass line for "It Could Happen to You" in G major. Transfer the melody to manuscript paper; abandon the melody and play dominant scales on all dominant chords as indicated in symbol key. ($x^{\sharp 3}$ also employs the normal dominant scale.)

Fig. 2.

$$(G) \quad I \;/\; III\phi \overset{M \text{ of } A}{VIx} \;/\; II \;/\; \flat V\phi \;/\; \overset{M \text{ of } B}{VIIx} \;/\; III \overset{M \text{ of } E\flat}{\flat IIIx} \;/\; II \; II_2 \;/$$

$$(G) \quad \overset{M \text{ of } B\flat}{\flat VIIx} \;/\; \overset{M \text{ of } A}{VIx} \;/\; II \;/\; II_2 \;/\; VIIm \;/\; \overset{M \text{ of } B\flat}{\flat VIIx} \;/\; VI^{\sharp\sharp 7} \; VI^{\sharp 7} \;/$$

$$(G) \quad VI \; \flat IIIo \;/\; II \; III \;/\; IV \overset{M \text{ of } G}{V} \;/\; I \;/\; III\phi \overset{M \text{ of } A}{VIx} \;/\; II \;/$$

$$(G) \quad \flat V\phi \overset{M \text{ of } B}{VIIx} \;/\; III \overset{M \text{ of } E\flat}{\flat IIIx} \;/\; II \; II_2 \;/\; \overset{M \text{ of } B\flat}{\flat VIIx} \overset{M \text{ of } A}{VIx} \;/\; II \; III \;/$$

$$(G) \quad IV^{\flat 3} \overset{M \text{ of } B\flat}{\flat VIIx} \;/\; I \overset{M \text{ of } F}{IVx} \;/\; III\phi \overset{M \text{ of } A}{VIx} \;/\; II \; III \;/\; IVm \overset{M \text{ of } G}{V} \;/$$

$$(G) \quad I^{+6} \;/\; I^{+6} \;//$$

IT COULD HAPPEN TO YOU — by Johnny Burke and Jimmy Van Heusen
© 1944 Famous Music Corp., New York, N. Y.

LESSON 44.

The Minor Scale

The minor chord in any key appears on II, III and VI.

CHORD	DISPLACEMENT	MODE
II	2 - 2	Dorian
III	3 - 3	Phrygian
VI	6 - 6	Aeolian

In a chord series with a strong key feeling,

I - VI - II - V - I   (Fig. 1)

or

II - III - IV - V - VI - II - V - I   (Fig. 2)

the three modes are used in their respective positions. There is never a question concerning the II chord since it belongs to a primary function of any key — II - V - I or II - $\flat$IIx - I. Therefore, II always takes the Dorian mode (2 - 2).

Fig. 1.

Fig. 2.

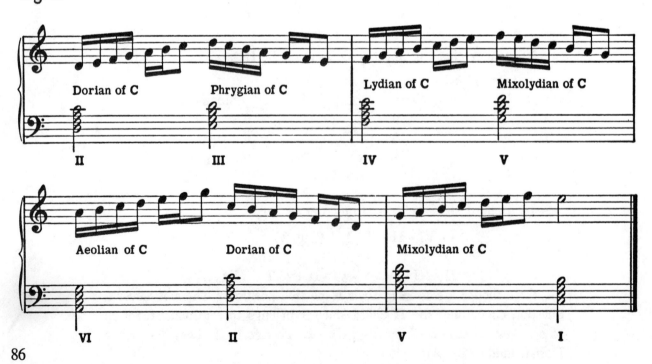

III and VI on the other hand, can easily be dislodged from a key center and therefore must be treated with more care. In such cases, III or VI become temporary II's of a new key and take the Dorian mode of that key.

Fig. 3 illustrates examples of III or VI becoming the temporary II of a new key.

Fig. 3.

Ionian of C   Lydian of C   Mixolydian of E   Dorian of D (temporary II)

I   IV   VIIx   III

Dorian of Eb   Mixolydian of Eb   Dorian of D (temporary II)   Mixolydian of D   Dorian of G (temporary II)

IVm   bVIIx   III   VIx   VI

All other minor chords (IVm, VIIm, bIII) are also treated as a temporary II of a new key. Thus, in the key of C:

CHORD	SPELLING	SCALE OR KEY	DISPLACEMENT
Im	Temporary II	Bb	C - C
II	Natural II	C	D - D
III	Natural III	C	E - E
III—when key center is weakened	Temporary II	D	E - E
IVm	Temporary II	Eb	F - F
Vm	Temporary II	F	G - G
VI	Natural VI	C	A - A
VI—when key center is weakened	Temporary II	G	A - A
VIIm	Temporary II	A	B - B
bIII	Temporary II	Db	Eb - Eb
bII	Temporary II	B	C# - C#

Except III and VI which usually take the Phrygian and Aeolian modes, respectively, all minor chords take the Dorian mode (2 - 2).

Where there is a strong diatonic feeling of the prevailing key, as in Fig. 1 and Fig. 2, the III chord takes the Phrygian mode and the VI chord takes the Aeolian mode.

When the prevailing key feeling is dislodged, as in Fig. 3, the III becomes a II of a new key and so also with the VI chord.

In jazz harmony, temporary II chords of other keys sometimes resolve to their natural dominants (V), but regardless of their resolution, at the moment they are played, they imply the II of a new key.

Actually the responsibility should rest with the student in deciding the particular "status" of the III or VI chord. The following rule, however, is a general guide to the use of the minor scale:

RULE: *The minor chord is a II or the temporary II of a new key and takes the scale of that key from root to root. The exceptions are III and VI, which normally take the Phrygian and Aeolian modes, respectively, when preceded by primary functions. If preceded by secondary or tertiary functions, both the III and VI chords become temporary II chords of another key.*

Fig. 4 illustrates the twelve minor chords with their accompanying Dorian modes, to be played ascending and descending.

Fig. 4.

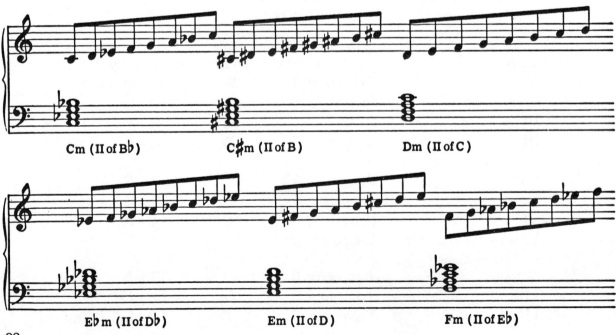

Cm (II of B♭)   C♯m (II of B)   Dm (II of C)

E♭m (II of D♭)   Em (II of D)   Fm (II of E♭)

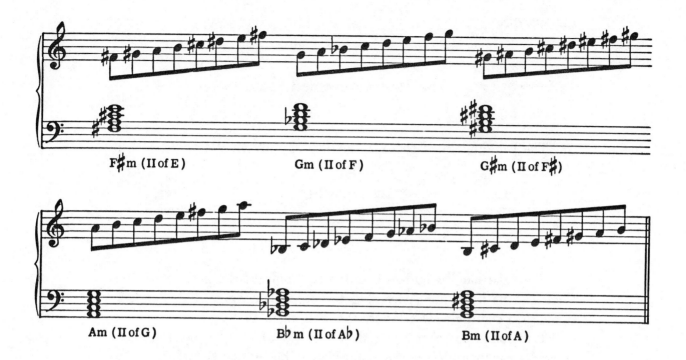

F♯m (II of E)   Gm (II of F)   G♯m (II of F♯)

Am (II of G)   B♭m (II of A♭)   Bm (II of A)

Fig. 5 is a bass line for "Little Girl Blue" in the key of F. Transfer the melody to manuscript paper; abandon the melody and play minor scales on all minor chords. The letters appearing over these chords indicate the signature to be played from root to root of the chord. For example: in bar 1, the F over VI means play the F scale from D to D; in bar 4, the B♭ over Vm means play the B♭ scale from C to C.

Fig. 5

$$I^{+6} \overset{F}{VI} / \overset{F}{II} bIIx / I^{+6} \overset{F}{VI} / \overset{Bb}{Vm} bV / IV IV^{+6} / \overset{Ab}{IVm} bVIIx /$$

$$IIIx^{\sharp 5} \overset{C}{VI} / \overset{F}{\underline{II}} \overset{F}{\underline{III}} IV \sharp IV\phi / V bV / \overset{F6}{II^5} \overset{F}{III} \overset{F}{II} bIIx / I^{+6} bIIIo /$$

$$\overset{F}{II} bIIM / I^{+6} \overset{F}{VI} / \overset{F}{II} bIIx / I^{+6} \overset{F}{VI} / \overset{Bb}{Vm} bV / IV IV^{+6} /$$

$$\overset{Ab}{IVm} bVIIx / IIIx^{\sharp 5} \overset{C}{VI} / \overset{F}{II} III \overset{F}{IV^{+6}} \sharp IV\phi / V bV /$$

$$\overset{F6}{II^5} \overset{F}{III} \overset{F}{II} bIIx / I^{+6} \sharp I / \bar{I}^{+6} \overset{F}{\underline{VI}} b\underline{VI}x / V / \overset{F}{II} bIIx / I \overset{F}{II} /$$

$$\overset{F}{III} IV / \overset{D}{VIIm} IIIx / \overset{D}{VIIm} bVIIx / \overset{C}{VI} V\phi / bV\phi IVo /$$

$$\overset{F*4}{VI^3} bIIIo / \overset{F}{II} bIIx / I^{+6} / I^{+6} //$$

LITTLE GIRL BLUE—by Richard Rodgers and Lorenz Hart

*NOTE: The prevailing key (F) has been reinstated despite the preceding *secondary function* in order to prepare for the final closing.

LESSON 45.

The Half-diminished Scale

The half-diminished chord in any key appears on VII only.

CHORD	DISPLACEMENT	MODE
VII	7 - 7	Locrian

Since the half-diminished chord occurs only at the position of VII, there can be no doubt concerning the accompanying mode. The half-diminished chord always takes the Locrian mode (7 - 7).

Half-diminished chords on other than VII (IIIϕ, bVϕ, etc.) are considered a temporary VII of some other key. Thus, in the key of C:

CHORD	SPELLING	SCALE OR KEY	DISPLACEMENT
Iϕ	Temporary VII	Db	C - C
IIϕ	Temporary VII	Eb	D - D
IIIϕ	Temporary VII	F	E - E
IVϕ	Temporary VII	Gb	F - F
Vϕ	Temporary VII	Ab	G - G
VIϕ	Temporary VII	Bb	A - A
VII	Natural VII	C	B - B
bIIIϕ	Temporary VII	E	D# - D#

In jazz harmony, the temporary half-diminished chord seldom, if ever, reaches its natural resolution, but at the moment it is played it implies the VII of a new key. Fig. 1 illustrates the twelve half-diminished chords with accompanying Locrian modes, to be played ascending and descending.

Fig. 1.

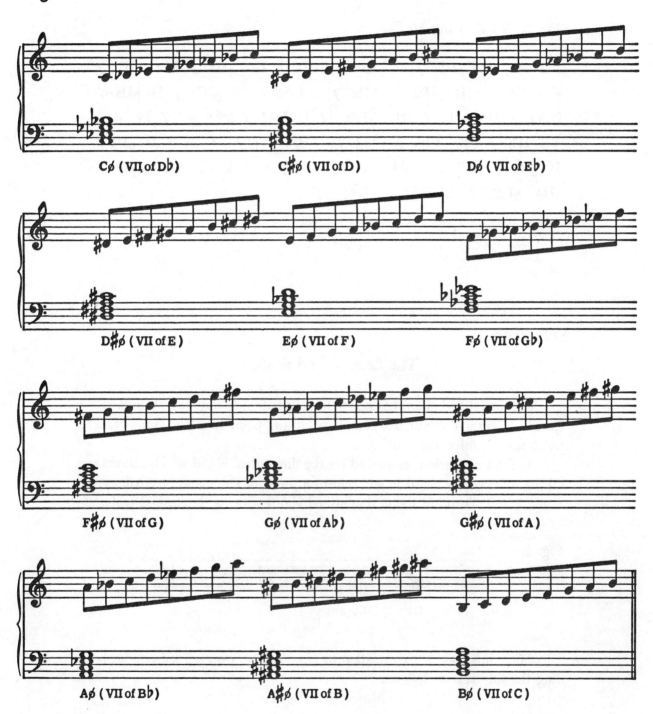

Fig. 2 is a bass line for "Don't Blame Me." Transfer the melody to manuscript paper. Abandon the melody and play appropriate half-diminished scales for each half-diminished chord.

Fig. 2. "Don't Blame Me."

I IVm / III ♭IIIx / II ♭IIx / I VI / IIφ ♭IIx / IIIφ ♭IIIx /

♭Vφ IVφ / III ♭IIIx II ♭IIx / I IVm / III ♭IIIx / II ♭IIx /

I VI / IIφ ♭IIx / IIIφ ♭IIIx / II V#³ / I+⁶ ♭V / IV II /

VII IIIx / VII ♭VIIx / VI#⁷ VI / IIx ♯Vo / VI IIx / II ♭III /

II ♭IIx / I IVm / III ♭IIIx / II ♭IIx / I VI / IIφ ♭IIx /

IIIφ ♭IIIx / II V#³ / I+⁶ //

LESSON 46.

The Diminished Scale

The diminished chord has no "natural" position in any key. We have learned to employ the diminished chord at any point in a key, but at no point does it infer any tonality.

An arbitrary scale is employed for the diminished chord which utilizes all the tones of the chord in addition to a series of chromatic or auxiliary tones. Fig. 1 illustrates the C diminished chord with its diminished scale.

Fig. 1.

Co   Co scale

Since this scale has no relation to any tonality, we spell it by indicating the intervals as follows:

Minor second — 1
Major second — 2

Thus, in Fig. 1, the semitone combination is:

C	D	E♭	F	G♭	A♭	A	B	C	
0	2	1	2	1	2	1	2	1	or 0 2 1 2 1 2 1 2 1

This is an artificial scale since the same letter, in any form (A♭ - A), cannot appear twice in an authentic scale.

Fig. 2 illustrates the twelve diminished chords with accompanying scales, to be played ascending and descending. The fingerings are a suggestion for the student.

Fig. 2.

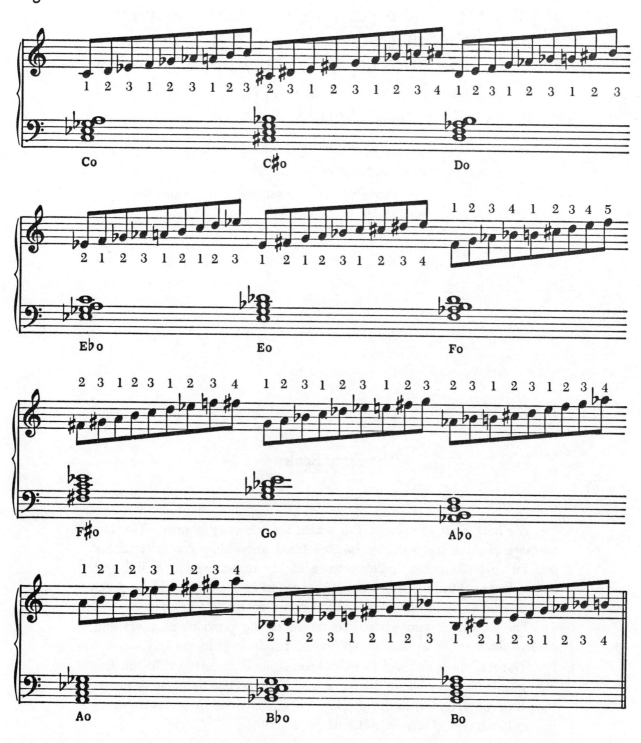

Fig. 3 is a bass line for "Birth of the Blues." Transfer the melody to manuscript paper. Abandon the melody and play diminished scales on all diminished chords.

Fig. 3.

^{pick-up}
♭IIx // I ♯Io / II ♯IIo / III IIIx♯⁵ / IV ♯IVo / V IV III ♭III /

II ♭IIx / I ⁺⁶ VI / II ♭IIx / I ♯Io / II ♯IIo / III IIIx♯⁵ /

IV ♯IVo / V IV III ♭III / II ♭IIx / I⁺⁶ ♯I / I⁺⁶ IVx /

IIIx VII / IIIx VII / IIIx IVx / IIIx / III VIx / III VIx /

VI IIx / II ♭IIx / I ♯Io / II ♯IIo / III IIIx♯⁵ / IV ♯IVo /

V IV III ♭III / II ♭IIx / I⁺⁶ / I⁺⁶ //

LESSON 47.

The Sixty Scales

We have now completed the scales for the sixty chords. The importance of these scales cannot be overstated in building the material for jazz improvisation. Fig. 1 illustrates a highly recommended drill based on the five qualities of each tone. These scales or modes should be practiced ascending and descending until they are completely automatic.

The student is also advised to return to the previous chapters and explore these scales in the various tunes abandoning the melody.

The student is advised to follow the general fingering rules for the major scales when playing the M, x, m and ϕ modes. Suggested fingerings have been added to the diminished scales since they represent an unfamiliar series of whole and half steps.

94

Fig. 1.

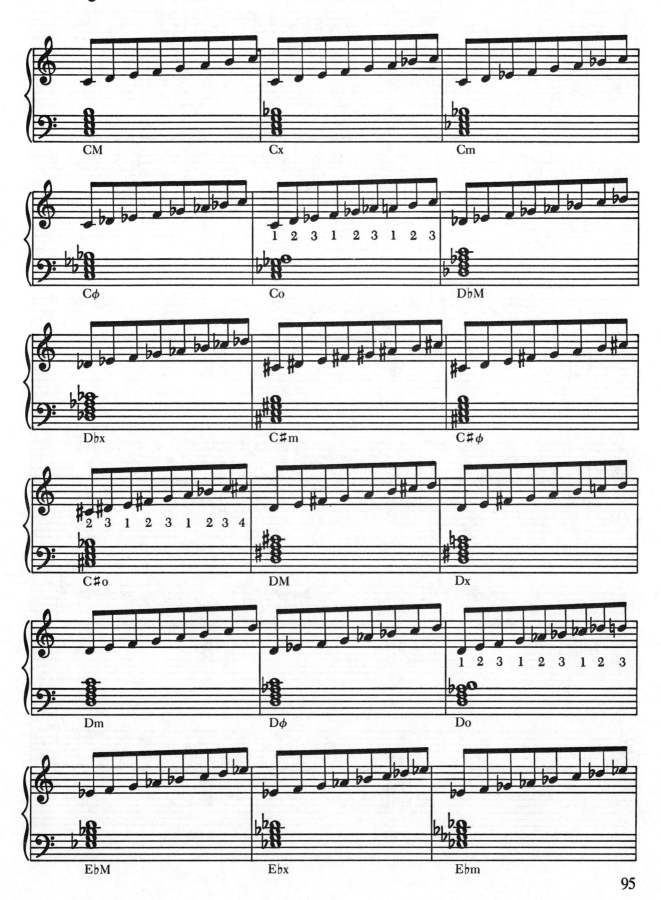

95

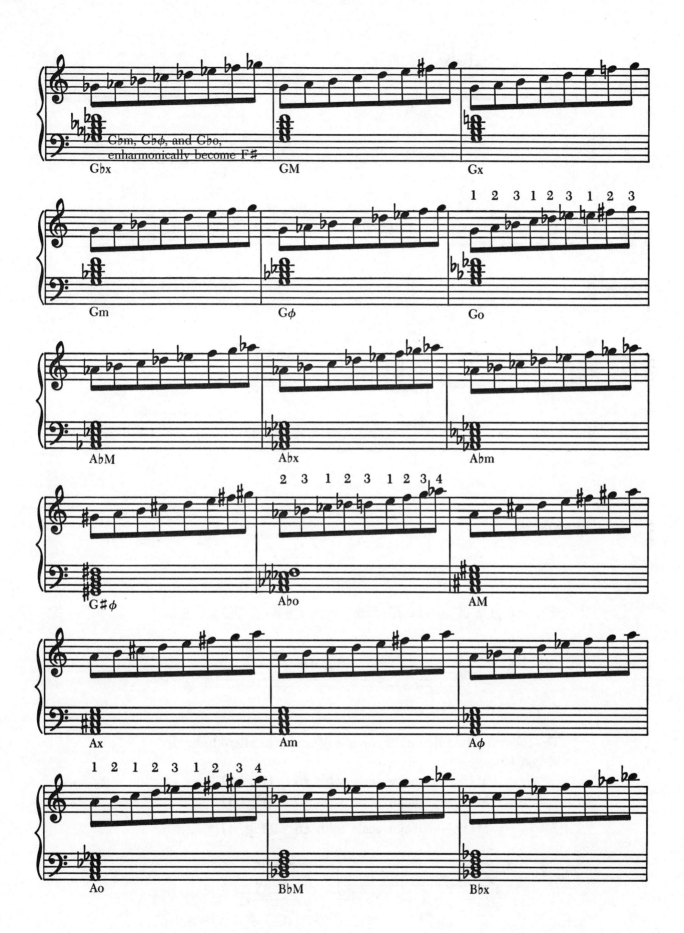

Gbx

Gbm, Gbϕ, and Gbo,
enharmonically become F#

GM

Gx

Gm

Gϕ

Go

1 2 3 1 2 3 1 2 3

AbM

Abx

Abm

G#ϕ

Abo

2 3 1 2 3 1 2 3 4

AM

Ax

Am

Aϕ

Ao

1 2 1 2 3 1 2 3 4

BbM

Bbx

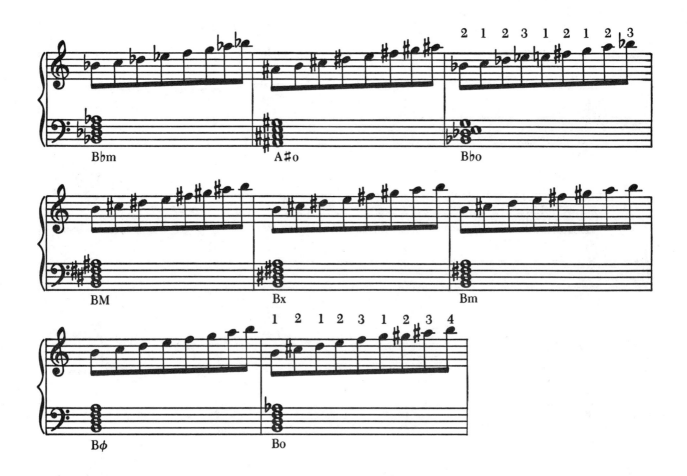

Bbm · A#o · Bbo · BM · Bx · Bm · Bφ · Bo

LESSON 48.

Scale and Arpeggio Alteration

The arpeggio of an altered chord simply follows the alteration.

Fig. 1.

Cm#7

The following rule describes the use of *scales* in altered chords:

MAJOR CHORD:

$M^{\#5}$ — major scale with #5 (Fig. 2)

M^{b5} — major scale with b5 (Fig. 3)

$M^{\#5}_{\#3}$ — major scale with #5 (Fig. 4)

Fig. 2.

CM#5

98

Fig. 3.

CM♭5

Fig. 4.

CM♯3♯5

DOMINANT CHORD:

x♯³	—	dominant scale	(Fig. 5)
x♯⁵	—	whole tone scale	(Fig. 6)
x♭⁵	—	whole tone scale	(Fig. 7)

Fig. 5.   Fig. 6.   Fig. 7.

Cx♯3   Cx♯5   Cx♭5

MINOR CHORD:

m♯♯⁷	—	minor scale	(Fig. 8)
m♯⁷	—	minor scale with ♯7	(Fig. 9)
m⁺⁶	—	minor scale	(Fig. 10)

Fig. 8.

Cm♯♯7

Fig. 9.   Fig. 10.   Fig. 11.

Cm♯7   Cm⁺6   Cx₂

RULE: *In inversions, the scale is the same as in root position except that it is played from the bottom note of the inversion (Fig. 11).*

Fig. 12 is a bass line for "Like Someone in Love" in the key of C. Transfer the melody to manuscript paper. Abandon the melody and play appropriate scales for the inversions. Letters over Roman numerals indicate the signature to be played from root to root (root position) or bass note to bass note (inversion). Thus in bar 1, $\overset{C}{I}_2$ indicates the scale of C from B to B; in bar 3, $\overset{C\ 4}{VII^3}$ indicates the scale of C from F to F.

Fig. 12. "Like Someone in Love."

(C) I $\overset{C}{I}_2$ / VI $\overset{C}{VI}_2$ / $\overset{G\,6}{IIx^5}$ $\overset{C\,4}{VII^3}$ / III $\flat$IIIx / II $\overset{E\flat\,4}{II\phi^3}$ /

(C) V $\flat$IIx / I VI / Vm $\flat$V / IV$^{+\,6}$ $\overset{F}{IV}_2$ / (A) $\overset{A}{II}_2$ VIIo /

(A) I $\overset{A}{I}_2$ / VI $\overset{A}{VI}_2$ / (C) VI $\overset{G\sharp\,7}{VI\sharp^7_2}$ / $\overset{G}{VI}_2$ $\flat$IIIo / II /

(C) $\flat$IIx / I $\overset{C}{I}_2$ / VI $\overset{C}{VI}_2$ / $\overset{G\,6}{IIx^5}$ $\overset{C\,4}{VII^3}$ / III $\flat$IIIx /

(C) II $\overset{E\flat\,4}{II\phi^3}$ / V $\flat$IIx / I VI / Vm $\flat$V / IV$^{+\,6}$ $\overset{F}{IV}_2$ /

(A) $\overset{A}{II}_2$ VIIo / I $\flat$V / (C) IIx $\sharp$IIo / III $\flat$IIIx / II $\flat$IIx /

(C) I$^{+\,6}$ / I$^{+\,6}$ //

LIKE SOMEONE IN LOVE—by Burke and Van Heusen
    © 1944 by Burke & Van Heusen, Inc. © renewed and assigned to Bourne Co. & Dorsey Bros. Music, Inc.
    Used by permission.

LESSON 49.

Eighth-note Scales—Scale Fragments

In Lesson 33, we moved to the primary step in improvising by abandoning the melody and playing eighth-note arpeggios on the chords. We will now repeat this primary step with eighth-note scales.

Fig. 1 illustrates the use of an eighth-note scale line. In playing Fig. 1, the student will notice the harsh sound (particularly on the M and x) of the scale fragment ending on the fourth note of the scale or the mode.

Fig. 1.

I   VI   II   V

To avoid this, in Fig. 2, the fourth step is removed and the tone row 1 2 3 5 is used (1 2 3 5 is always counted from the root of the chord).

Fig. 2.

     I   VI   II   V

Fig. 3 illustrates the scale fragments on 5 4 3 1 (reverse of 1 2 3 5).

Fig. 3.

     Ix   VIx   IIx   V

Fig. 4 illustrates the scale fragments on 3 4 5 7.

Fig. 4.

     Im   VIx   IIx   V

Fig. 5 illustrates the scale fragments on 7 6 5 3.

Fig. 5.

     Iø   VIx   IIø   V

Fig. 6 illustrates the scale fragments on 5 6 7 2.

Fig. 6.

     Io   *   VIo   IIo   V

°The fragment figures for the diminished scale are not the same since the diminished scale consists of eight tones rather than the usual seven. The fragment figures for the diminished scale are as follows:

$$1\ 2\ 3\ 5\ -\ 5\ 4\ 3\ 1\ \text{ (reverse)}$$
$$3\ 4\ 5\ 7\ -\ 7\ 6\ 5\ 3\ \text{ (reverse)}$$
$$5\ 6\ 7\ 1\ -\ 1\ 8\ 7\ 5\ \text{ (reverse)}$$

Fig. 7 illustrates the scale fragments on 2 1 7 5; and 1 8 7 5 (diminished).

Fig. 7.

All of these fragments are of the utmost importance in using scale lines; the ability to pick up any scale fragment for any chord is an absolute prerequisite for improvising facility.

Inversions take the scale of the root position chord from bass note to bass note of the inversion. See below.

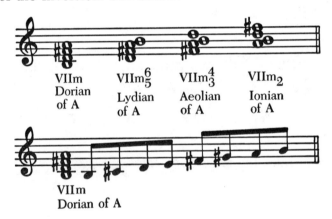

Fig. 8 is a bass line for "Blue Moon," in the key of E. Transfer the melody to manuscript paper noting key changes, using three staves as in previous lessons. Play or write out a line using eighth-note scale fragments of the chords.

Fig. 8.

pick-up
(E) $\flat$IIx // I VI / II $\flat$IIx / I VI / II IIϕ / III VI /

(E) II V$^{\sharp 3}$ / $\hat{1}^{+6}$ $\flat$IIIo / II $\flat$IIx / I VI / II $\flat$IIx /

(E) I VI / II IIϕ / III VI / II V$^{\sharp 3}$ / I^{+6} $\sharp$I / I VI /

(E) II $\flat$IIx / I^{+6} VI / II $\flat$IIx / I^{+6} VI / (G) II $\flat$IIx /

(G) I VI / (E) VIIm III VI IIx / II $\flat$IIx / I VI / II $\flat$IIx /

(E) I VI / II IIϕ / III VI / II V$^{\sharp 3}$ / I^{+6} / I^{+6} //

Fig. 9 illustrates a drill on Fig. 8 using the various fragments.

FRAGMENT CHART

FRAGMENT					REVERSE			
1	2	3	5		5	4	3	1
3	4	5	7		7	6	5	3
5	6	7	2		2	1	7	5

Fig. 9.

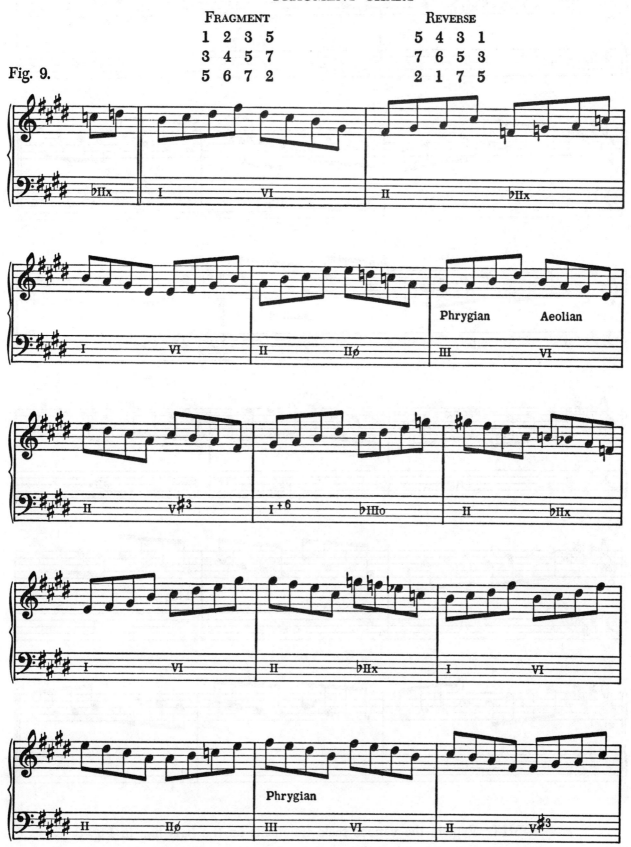

103

DRILL: Explore the various scale fragments on the bass line in Fig. 8.
Keep a steady quarter-note foot beat.

Eighth-note Triplet Scale Fragments

Fig. 1 is a bass line for "Cabin in the Sky," in the key of G. The eighth-note triplet line should be considered here. This means three notes to a beat or six notes to each half-note chord. Transfer the melody to manuscript paper using three staves. Note key change. Write out or play a line using eighth-note triplet scale fragments on the bass line in Fig. 1 with a quarter-note foot beat.

Fig. 1.

(G) I ♯Iφ / II ♯IIo / IIIφ / ♭IIIx / II♯♯⁷ II♯⁷ /

(G) II IVo / III ♭IIIx / II ♭IIx / I ♯Iφ / II ♯IIo /

(G) IIIφ / ♭IIIx / II♯♯⁷ II♯⁷ / II ♭IIx / I⁺⁶ ♯I / I⁺⁶ IV /

(G) VIIm ♭VIIx / VI⁺⁶ ♭Vφ / (E) II ♭IIx / I / (G) VI♯♯⁷ VI♯⁷ /

(G) VI IIx / V IV / III II / I ♯Iφ / II ♯IIo / IIIφ /

(G) ♭IIIx / II♯♯⁷ II♯⁷ / II ♭IIx / I⁺⁶ / I⁺⁶ //

Fig. 2 illustrates a drill using scale fragments in eighth-note triplets.

Fig. 2.

VIIm   ♭VIIx   VI +6   ♭Vø

II   ♭IIx   I

VI #7   VI #7   VI   IIx

Lydian   Phrygian

V   IV   III   II

I   #Iø   II   #IIo

IIIø   ♭IIIx

106

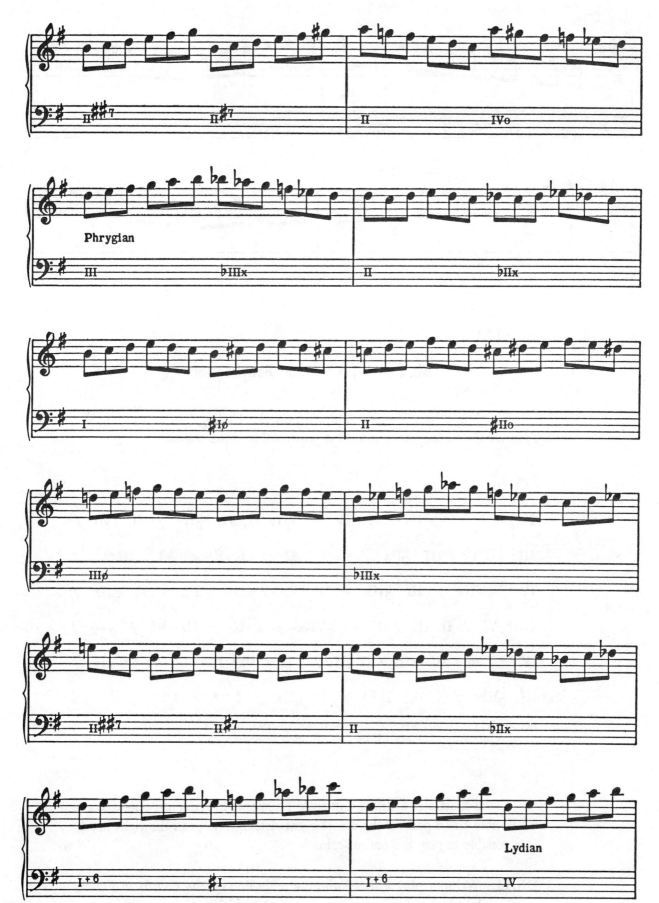

LESSON 51.

Sixteenth-note Scale Fragments

Fig. 1 is a bass line for "Dancing on the Ceiling," in the key of F. Transfer the melody to manuscript paper using three staves.

Fig. 1.

I II / VI$\frac{4}{3}$ IIIx$^{\sharp 5}$ / IV^{+6} VIIx / III ♭III / II IVo /

III ♭IIIx / II ♭IIx / I^{+6} ♯I / I II / VI$\frac{4}{3}$ IIIx$^{\sharp 5}$ /

IV^{+6} VIIx / III ♭III / II IVo / III ♭IIIx / II ♭IIx /

I^{+6} VI / II III / IV^{+6} ♭VIIx / I II / III VI / ♭Vø /

IV^{+6} IVm / III ♭IIIx / II ♭IIx / I II / VI$\frac{4}{3}$ IIIx$^{\sharp 5}$ / IV^{+6} VIIx /

III ♭IIIx / II$^{\sharp\sharp 7}$ II$^{\sharp 7}$ / II ♭IIx / I^{+6} / I^{+6} //

DANCING ON THE CEILING—Lyrics by Lorenz Hart, Music by Richard Rodgers
    © 1930 (renewed) Warner Bros. Inc. All rights reserved.
    Used by permission.

Fig. 2 illustrates a drill using scale fragments in sixteenth notes. Since a half-note chord permits the use of eight sixteenth notes in the right hand, it is possible to play the entire scale.

DRILL: Write or play a sixteenth-note scale line on the chords in Fig. 1, keeping a steady quarter-note foot beat.

108

Fig. 2.

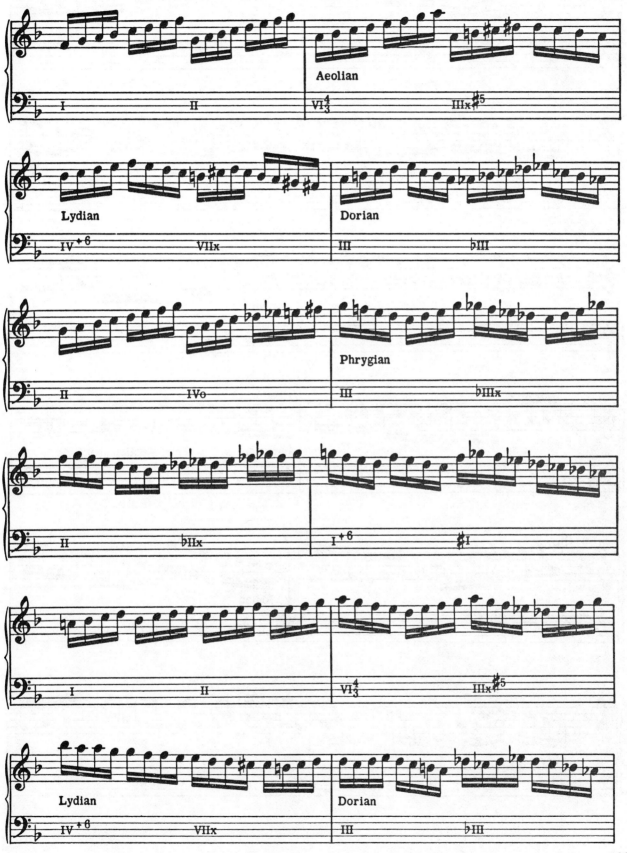

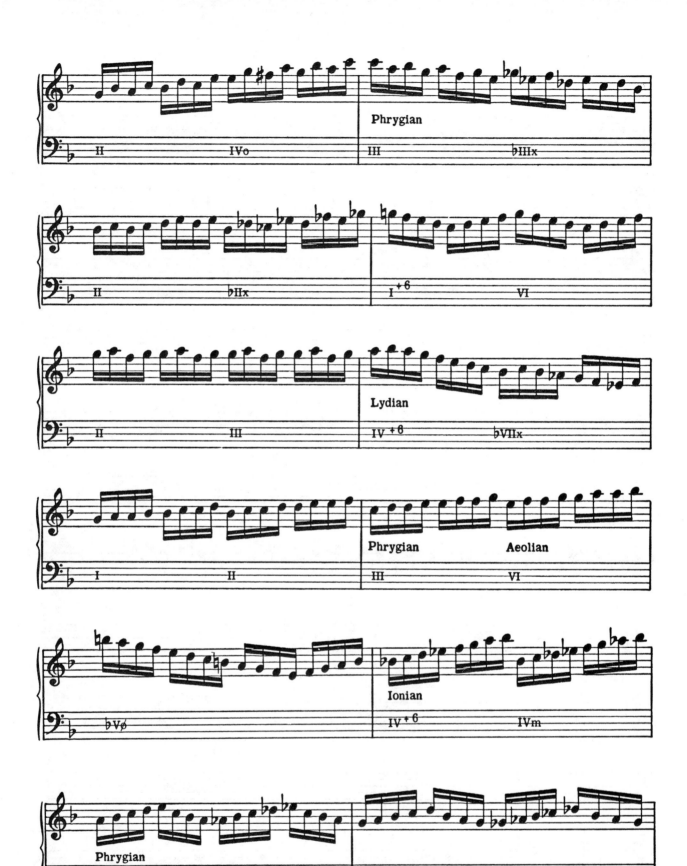

LESSON 52.

Rhythmic Combinations

As in Lesson 38, when treating arpeggios, we will now proceed to combine the rhythm values using the scales as a framework.

Fig. 1 is a bass line for "Round Midnight," in the key of Eb minor. Transfer the melody to manuscript paper using three staves and noting key changes.

Fig. 1

(G♭) VI VI₂ / ♭V͡ó V͡II ♭V͡IIx / VI IIx / IV͡m ♭V͡IIx I͡II V͡Ix /

(G♭) II V / I IIx^♭5 / ♭Vφ VIIx / IIIx ♭VIIx / VI VI₂ /

(G♭) ♭V͡ó V͡II ♭V͡IIx / VI IIx / IV͡m ♭V͡IIx I͡II V͡Ix / II V / I IIx^♭5 //

(E♭) V͡Iφ I͡Ix V͡^♯3 ♭I͡Ix / I^+6 / VIφ IIx / V ♭IIx / VIφ IIx / V Ix //

(G♭) I͡I I͡I₂ V͡II I͡IIx / ♭V͡φ V͡IIx I͡II V͡Ix / I͡I V͡ I͡m IV͡x /

(G♭) ♭V͡IIm ♭I͡IIx V͡II ♭V͡IIx / V͡I V͡I₂ / ♭V͡ó V͡II ♭V͡IIx / VI IIx /

(G♭) IVm ♭VIIx III VIx / II V / I IIx^♭5 // (E♭) V͡Iφ I͡Ix V͡^♯3 ♭I͡Ix /

(E♭) I^+6 //

'ROUND MIDNIGHT—Lyrics by Bernie Hanighen, Music by Cootie Williams and
Thelonious Monk

Fig. 2 illustrates a drill employing eighth-note, eighth-note triplet and
sixteenth-note values.

Fig. 2.

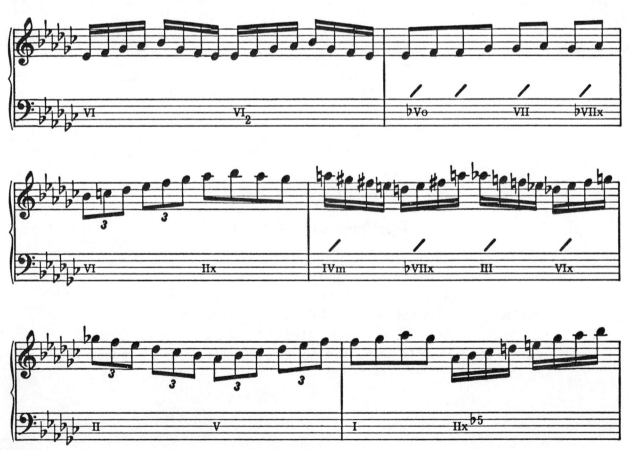

DRILL: Write out or play a scale line on Fig. 1 using eighth-note, eighth-note triplet and sixteenth-note values.

LESSON 53.

Rhythmic Composite (ballad)

Just as we abandoned the melody in Lessons 30 and 40 and applied the arpeggios to a rhythmic composite, we will now apply the scales of the chords using the same process.

Fig. 1 is a rhythmic composite for a ballad.

Fig. 1.

Fig. 2 is a bass line for "Have You Met Miss Jones?" in the key of F. Transfer the melody to manuscript paper using three staves. Note key changes.

Fig. 2.

(F) I / #Io / II / IVo / III VI / IIx♭⁵ / II / ♭IIx / I / #Io /

(F) II / IVo / III VI / IIx♭⁵ / II V / (B♭) II ♭IIx / I VI /

(G♭) II ♭IIx / I VI / (D) II ♭IIx / I VI / (G♭) II ♭IIx / I /

(F) II ♭IIx / I / #Io / II / V / ♭Vm ♭IIIo / II ♭IIx / I⁺⁶ / I⁺⁶ //

Fig. 3 is a drill applying the scales of the bass line in Fig. 2 to the composite in Fig. 1. In each case the required mode has been followed, although the starting point of each phrase has not necessarily been the root of the chord. Each note of the mode becomes a possible starting or ending point.

Using Fig. 3 as a model, play or write out an improvisation using the composite and the scales of the bass line in Fig. 2.

Fig. 3.

117

118

Rhythmic Composite (up-tempo)

As in the arpeggio study, the composite is simplified in up-tempo tunes to insure a stronger feeling of swing. Fig. 1 is a possible composite for an up-tempo tune.

Fig. 1.

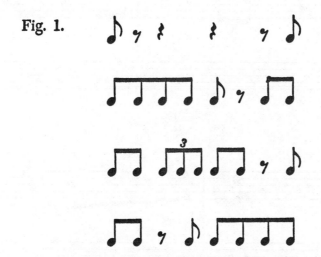

Fig. 2 is a bass line for "Lullaby of Birdland," in the key of B. Transfer the melody to manuscript paper using three staves.

Fig. 2.

VI^{+6} ♭Vϕ / VIIx IIIx / VI$^{♯7}$ VI / II IVo / III VI / II V /
I IV / VII IIIx / VI^{+6} ♭Vϕ / VIIx IIIx / VI$^{♯7}$ VI / II IVo /
III VI / II V / I ♭IIx / I^{+6} / IIIϕ ♭IIIx / II / IIϕ ♭IIx /
I / IIIϕ ♭IIIx / II / IIϕ ♭IIx / I IV VII IIIx / VI^{+6} ♭Vϕ /
VIIx IIIx / VI$^{♯7}$ VI / II IVo / III VI / II V / I ♭IIx / I^{+6} //

Fig. 3 is a drill based on Figs. 1 and 2. The student will notice the extensive use of rest values in Fig. 1. Silence also swings. The beginner will tend to play too many notes but should strive for the "punctuation" that characterizes a good line.

Fig. 3.

121

LESSON 55.

The Chromatic Tones

In the previous chapters we have studied the following elements of the twelve tones in the octave:

1. Arpeggio — four tones of the octave
2. Scale — seven tones of the octave except diminished

Now we must consider the remaining five tones of the M, x, m and φ scales and the remaining four tones of the diminished scale.

Fig. 1 illustrates the five qualities on C with the accompanying scales.

Fig. 1.

The following table indicates the omitted tones in each scale:

CM: Db - Eb - Gb - Ab - Bb
Cx: Db - Eb - Gb - Ab - B
Cm: Db - E - Gb - Ab - B
Cφ: D - E - G - A - B
Co: Db - E - G - Bb

It is a good rule in jazz improvisation to avoid more than four consecutive chromatic tones. The chromatic scale involves all twelve tones and therefore cannot infer any specific chord.

One of the most effective ways of utilizing the chromatic tones is as follows.
1. Treat the root, third, fifth, seventh and ninth as principal tones.
2. In approaching a chord, choose one of the principal tones as a "target" note.
3. Pass through the chromatic tones a minor second each side of the "target" note, then into the "target" note.

CHORD	PRINCIPAL TONES	CHROMATIC TONES
II	D	C# — Eb
	F	E — Gb
	A	G# — Bb
	C	B — Db
	E	D# — F
V	G	F# — Ab
	B	A# — C
	D	C# — Eb
	F	E — Gb
	A	G# — Bb
I	C	B — Db
	E	D# — F
	G	F# — Ab
	B	A# — C
	D	C# — Eb

The chromatic tones may move in either direction before resolving to the principal tone although modern idioms prefer the descending form:

Eb — C# into D   Db — B into C
Gb — E into F   F — D# into E
Bb — G# into A

Fig. 2 is a bass line for "I Cover the Waterfront," in the key of G. Transfer the melody to manuscript paper using three staves and noting key changes.

Fig. 2.

(G) VI IIx♭⁵ / II ♭IIx / I II / III ♭IIIo / II VI⁴₃ / II ♭IIx /

(G) I VIIx / ♭VIIx VIx / VI IIx♭⁵ / II ♭IIx / I II / III ♭IIIo /

(G) II VI⁴₃ / II ♭IIx / I⁺⁶ ♯I / I⁺⁶ VI / II IVo / III ♭IIIx /

(G) II ♭IIx / I I⁺⁶ / (A) II IVo / III VI / II ♭IIx /

(G) II II₂ VII ♭VIIx / VI IIx♭⁵ / II ♭IIx / I II / III ♭IIIo /

(G) II VI⁴₃ / II ♭IIx / I⁺⁶ / I⁺⁶ //

I COVER THE WATERFRONT—Lyrics by Edward Heyman, Music by Johnny Green
© 1933 (renewed) Warner Bros. Inc. All rights reserved.
Used by permission.

Fig. 3 illustrates the use of chromatic tones in a scale-arpeggio drill with no particular rhythmic pattern. Using this figure as a model, write or play an improvised line on the chords of Fig. 2 using chromatic elements.

Fig. 3.

The Sensitive Tones

We have now studied sufficient jazz material to understand the basic tonal principles of the art form.

Jazz employs a sixty chord harmonic system over which is played a twelve-tone melodic line. Fig. 1 illustrates the vertical movement of jazz harmony referred to in Lesson 1, Fig. 2.

Fig. 1.

We have given careful study to the root, third, fifth and seventh; we will now consider the ninth, eleventh and thirteenth in relation to the five basic qualities (major, dominant, minor, half-diminished and diminished).

Chord Quality	Sensitive Tones
Major	9 - $\sharp$11
Dominant	9 - $\flat$9 - $\sharp$9
	11 ($\sharp$3) - $\sharp$11
	13 - $\flat$13
Minor	9 - 11
Half-diminished	9 - 11
Diminished	9 - 11

See Fig. 2.

Fig. 2.

CM^9 CM$\sharp^{11}$ Cx^9 Cx$\flat^9$ Cx$\sharp^9$ Cx^{11}($\sharp$3) Cx$\sharp^{11}$

Cx^{13} $Cx^{\flat 13}$ Cm^9 Cm^{11} $C\varnothing^9$ $C\varnothing^{11}$ Co^9 Co^{11}

As part of a well conceived line, these tones can bring a tonal interest lacking in the root, third, fifth and seventh. By themselves, these tones are of little value; they are to be considered occasional tension points of a twelve-tone line.

Fig. 3 is a bass line for "Night and Day," in the key of E♭. Fig. 4 is a drill illustrating the use of the sensitive tones.

Transfer the melody to manuscript paper using three staves and noting key changes.

Fig. 3. "Night and Day."

pick-up
(E♭) I // ♭VIM / V / I / I⁺⁶ / ♭VIM / V / I / VI / ♭Vφ /

(E♭) IVm / III / ♭IIIo / II / ♭IIx / I / I / ♭VIM / V / I /

(E♭) I⁺⁶ / ♭VIM / V / I / VI / ♭Vφ / IVm / III / ♭IIIo / II /

(E♭) ♭IIx / I / I⁺⁶ / (G♭) I II / III I / (E♭) I II / III I /

(G♭) I II / III I / (E♭) I II / III VI / ♭Vφ / IVm / III /

(E♭) ♭IIIo / II / ♭IIM / I⁺⁶ / I⁺⁶ //

NIGHT AND DAY—Words and Music by Cole Porter

Play an improvised line on these chords employing the sensitive tones using the following Fig. 4 as a model.

Fig. 4.

131

LESSON 57.

Basic Syncopation

A thorough study of jazz syncopation is beyond the scope of this book. Jazz syncopation appears on many levels. Our concern is with syncopation in the improvised line. Fig. 1 illustrates a series of even eighth notes played against a quarter-note beat. Notes 1, 3, 5 and 7 are the "strong" points in Fig. 1. Notes 2, 4, 6 and 8 are the "weak" points. By tying the tones in Fig. 1 together, the "strong" points of the series are disrupted (Fig. 2). This is basic syncopation.

Fig. 1.

Fig. 2.

Fig. 3 is a bass line for "Easy To Love," in A♭. The sheet music appears in G and must be transposed to A♭. Transfer melody to manuscript paper using three staves. Write or play a line on Fig. 3 applying syncopation using Fig. 4, which illustrates this process, as a model.

Fig. 3.

II VII / III∅ ♭IIIx / II / ♭IIx / I / II / III / ♭IIIx / II /

V♯³ / I / ♯Io / II∅ / IV∅ / III / ♭IIIo / II VII / III∅ ♭IIIx /

II / ♭IIx / I / II / III / VIx / II III / IVm ♭VIIx / III /

♭IIIo / II / ♭IIx / I⁺⁶ / I⁺⁶ //

EASY TO LOVE—by Cole Porter

Fig. 4.

DRILL: Practice the sixty arpeggios in syncopated eighth notes as in
Fig. 5.

Fig. 5.

Foot beat

etc.

135

Practice the sixty scales in syncopated eighth notes (Fig. 6).

Fig. 6.

The study of both Figs. 5 and 6 should be accompanied by an un-interrupted quarter-note foot beat.

LESSON 58.

Accent

In addition to syncopation, the device of accent is valuable in creating rhythmic interest in a jazz line.

Fig. 1 illustrates the scale of C in eighth notes played with a quarter-note foot beat. Here, the accented tones fall on 1, 3, 5 and 7 which are also the accent points of the foot beat.

Fig. 1.

In Fig. 2, the accented tones fall on 2, 4, 6 and 8 which are struck while the foot is in the air. The student will find Fig. 1 easy to play. Fig. 2 will be troublesome in the beginning since the hand and the foot are in opposition to each other.

Fig. 2.

The use of accent in an eighth-note series, as in Fig. 2, is of the utmost importance in creating rhythmic interest in a jazz line and should be carefully studied by the pupil.

Fig. 3 is a bass line for "Makin' Whoopee," in the key of A.* Fig. 4 illustrates a drill on Fig. 3 employing the use of accent. Wedges over the tones indicate the accent points of the line.

Transfer the melody to manuscript paper using three staves. Write or play a line on Fig. 3 using Fig. 4 as a model.

Fig. 3.

pick-up

♭IIx // I ♯Io / II V / Vm Ix / IVm ♭VIIx / III VI / ♭III ♭VIx /

VI$^4_3$ ♭IIIo / II ♭IIx / I ♯Io / II V / Vm Ix / IVm ♭VIIx /

III VI / ♭III ♭VIx / I^{+6} II / ♯IIo VI$^4_3$ / Vm Ix / IV^{+6} /

IVm ♭VIIx / I II ♯IIo III / Vm Ix / IV^{+6} / IVm ♭VIIx /

III ♭IIIx II ♭IIx / I ♯Io / II V / Vm Ix / IVm ♭VIIx / III VI /

♭III ♭VIx / I^{+6} / I^{+6} //

MAKIN' WHOOPEE—Lyrics by Gus Kahn, Music by Walter Donaldson
U.S. © 1940 (renewed) Warner Bros. Music Corp. All rights reserved.
U.K. © 1928 Bregman, Vocco, and Conn Inc. Sub-published by Keith Prowse Music
Publishing Co. Ltd.
Used by permission.

Fig. 4.

*The sheet music appears in G, so melody must be transposed to A.

137

138

DRILL: Practice the sixty arpeggios in accented eighth notes as in Fig. 5.

Fig. 5.

Practice the sixty scales in accented eighth notes as in Fig. 6.

Fig. 6.

Both Figs. 5 and 6 should be accompanied by an uninterrupted quarter-note foot beat.

LESSON 59.

Coleman Hawkins' "Sweet Lorraine" in G

In the course of some fifty years of jazz, there are many recorded masterpieces of the improvised line: Book II will deal thoroughly with this aspect of jazz. Since the reproduction of one of these masterpieces can do much to reveal to the student all of the elements studied in this volume, Coleman Hawkins' "Sweet Lorraine" (originally recorded on Signature 90,001, reissued on Brunswick, LP BL54016) has been included here.

This recording involves two improvised choruses by Hawkins. These two choruses are undoubtedly one of the great moments in the history of jazz improvisation; they also employ every device described in this text. The student is strongly advised to make a thorough study of these two choruses using the following outline as a course of study.

1. Scale and arpeggio analysis.
2. Rhythmic values.
3. Rest values.
4. Syncopation.
5. Phrasing:
    (a) starting points.
    (b) the bar line.
    (c) contrast.
    (d) punctuation.
6. Chromaticism.
7. Accent.
8. Over-all architecture.

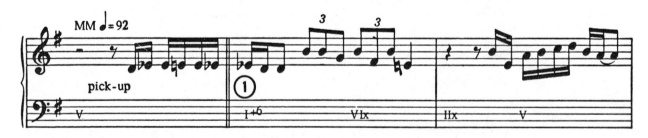

SWEET LORRAINE—by Parrish, Burwell

141

The following is a left hand stride solution to "Sweet Lorraine" with a new chord appearing on every beat of the tune. This is a paraphrase of a stride treatment of this tune by Art Tatum (originally recorded 2/22/40 on Decca Label 8715).

The following table explains the code used in this treatment:

10—Root, 7th, 10th (5-2-1 fingering)

7—Root, 3rd, 7th (4-2-1 fingering)

3rd Inversion $\frac{4}{2}$—7th, 3rd, 5th, Root (5-3-2-1 fingering)

2nd Inversion $\frac{4}{3}$—5th, Root 3rd, 7th (5-3-2-1 fingering)

This treatment employs all three spans (see Volume 3, page 18), and quick "rolling" may be essential for smaller hands.

Each tenth is individually pedaled.

On a first reading, the student will notice several tension points in relation to the melody and harmony, but as the forward motion begins to take place, these tension points will disappear.

pick-up

$\overset{10}{\flat IIx}$ / $\overset{10}{I}$ $\overset{10}{\flat VIIx}$ $\overset{10}{VIx}$ $\overset{10}{\sharp Io}$ / $\overset{10}{II}$ $\overset{4}{II^2}$ $\overset{10}{VII}$ $\overset{10}{\flat VIIx}$ / $\overset{10}{VI}$ $\overset{7}{IIx}$ $\overset{10}{Vm}$ $\overset{7}{Ix}$ /

$\overset{10}{Im}$ $\overset{7}{IVx}$ $\overset{10}{VII}$ $\overset{7}{IIIx}$ / $\overset{10}{III}$ $\overset{7}{VIx}$ $\overset{10}{\flat III\phi}$ $\overset{7}{\flat VIx}$ / $\overset{10}{II}$ $\overset{10}{III}$ $\overset{10}{IV}$ $\overset{10}{IVo}$ /

$\overset{10}{III}$ $\overset{7}{\flat VIIx}$ $\overset{7}{VIx}$ $\overset{10}{\flat IIIx}$ / $\overset{10}{II}$ $\overset{7}{\flat VIx}$ $\overset{7}{V}$ $\overset{10}{\flat IIx}$ / $\overset{10}{I}$ $\overset{10}{\flat VIIx}$ $\overset{10}{VIx}$ $\overset{10}{\sharp Io}$ /

$\overset{10}{II}$ $\overset{4}{II^2}$ $\overset{10}{VII}$ $\overset{10}{\flat VIIx}$ / $\overset{10}{VI}$ $\overset{7}{IIx}$ $\overset{10}{Vm}$ $\overset{7}{Ix}$ / $\overset{10}{Im}$ $\overset{7}{IVx}$ $\overset{10}{VII}$ $\overset{7}{IIIx}$ /

$\overset{10}{III}$ $\overset{7}{VIx}$ $\overset{10}{\flat III\phi}$ $\overset{7}{\flat VIx}$ / $\overset{10}{II}$ $\overset{10}{III}$ $\overset{10}{IV}$ $\overset{7}{V}$ / $\overset{10}{I}$ $\overset{4}{I^2}$ $\overset{}{VI}$ $\overset{}{\flat VI}$ /

Vm $\flat IIx$ Ix $\flat V$ /

bridge

IV^{10} $\flat\text{VIIM}^{7}$ III^{10} VIx^{7} / II^{10} V^{7} Im^{10} IVx^{7} / IV^{10} $\flat\text{VIIM}^{7}$ III^{10} VIx^{7} /

II^{10} V^{7} Im^{10} IVx^{7} / Ivm^{10} $\flat\text{VIIx}^{7}$ III^{10} VIx^{7} / $\flat\text{III}^{10}$ $\flat\text{VIx}^{7}$ II^{10} V^{7} /

IVm^{10} $\flat\text{VIIx}^{10}$ III^{10} VIx^{7} / $\flat\text{III}^{10}$ $\flat\text{VIx}^{7}$ II^{10} V^{7} / I^{10} $\flat\text{VIIx}^{10}$ VIx^{10} $\sharp\text{Io}^{10}$ /

II^{10} II^{4}_{2} VII^{10} $\flat\text{VIIx}^{10}$ / VI^{10} IIx^{7} Vm^{10} Ix^{7} / Im^{10} IVx^{7} VII^{10} IIIx^{7} /

III^{10} VIx^{7} $\flat\text{III}\phi^{10}$ $\flat\text{VIx}^{7}$ / II^{10} III^{10} IV^{10} V^{7} / I^{10} Ix^{3}_{4} $\flat\text{V}\phi^{10}$ IVm^{10} /

III^{10} II^{10} I^{10} $\natural$ //

SECTION VIII

LESSON 60.

The Blues (harmonic)

To a jazz musician, the blues means a fairly fixed set of chords or "changes." These chords have evolved from the archaic folk music of America and can be heard in the recordings of Blind Lemon Jefferson, Big Bill Broonzy and Leadbelly (Huddie Ledbetter). All jazz blues involve the I, IV and V chords in a 12-bar form.

From this prehistory of the archaic blues has slowly evolved a conventional set of chords which most musicians accept as representative. These chords are as follows:

Fig. 1.

Ix / IVx / Ix / Vm Ix / IVx / IVx / I II / III ♭IIIx / II V / II V //

$^{(1)}$I^{+6} ♭IIIo / II V :‖ $^{(2)}$Ī$^{+6}$ Īx$^{6}_{5}$ IV̄ ♯IV̄o / VI$_2$ ♭IIx Ix ₹ //

(2) represents the final close ending the blues and is traditionally called a *seven-beater* (seven beats to the end — the last beat is not played). Otherwise the first ending (1) is taken and the twelve bars are repeated over and over. In the second ending the rhythmic pattern of the final bars is as follows:

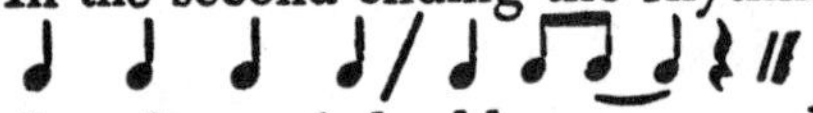

A more modern form of the blues was evolved by Charlie Parker in the forties and, while respecting the main "pivot" chords, this new form contains many harmonic sequences not found in the traditional form:

Fig. 2.

I^{+6} IV / VIIm IIIx$^{♭5}$ / VI IIx$^{♭5}$ / Vm Ix$^{♭5}$ / Im IVx / IVm ♭VIIx /

III / VIx$^{♭5}$ / II V / II V // $^{(1)}$I^{+6} ♭IIIM / ♭VIM V:‖

$^{(2)}$ I^{+6} ♭IIx / Ix$^{♭5}$ //

There is no "melody" for the blues. Many tunes using the term or title of blues are not "blues" in the sense referred to in this chapter; these tunes evoke a mood sometimes referred to as "blue" — this is a poetic reference, not a musicological one.

Transfer Figs. 1 and 2 to manuscript paper and write or play an improvisation on the chord changes. Explore Figs. 1 and 2 in twelve keys.

LESSON 61.

The Blues (melodic)

The melodic aspect of the blues is of much greater significance than the isolated chord charts studied in Lesson 60. A strong feeling of the blues has characterized all great melodic improvisation. In this sense the blues represent, along with ragtime, the basic substrata of all jazz.

The basic idea of melodic blues lies in the "twang" of the sliding and crushed tones present in all archaic guitar. These inflected tones have been simulated on all jazz instruments including the piano. Of all the instruments, the piano is in many ways the least effective in creating a blues feeling since once a tone is struck it cannot be changed or even sustained for any length of time.

On the piano, "blue" tones are usually achieved by crushing one tone into another (Fig. 1). Because of the physical structure of the keyboard, the most effective positions are those in which a black note can be crushed into a white note [(b) and (c) in Fig. 1]. The reason for this is that the same finger can be used for both tones by applying an arm stroke to the tones. This is called *false fingering*. This is impossible in (a) of Fig. 1 which requires two fingers to execute.

Fig. 1.

(a)   (b)   (c)

This principle can be extended to two or more tones played simultaneously.

Fig. 2.

In any interval, one tone (usually the lower) can be crushed while the second is held (Fig. 3).

Fig. 3.

The most familiar sound associated with these crushed tones is that of the augmented ninth crushed into the major third when playing a dominant chord.

Fig. 4.

These devices can become tiresome if not supported by an otherwise interesting line; used occasionally they can be effective in bringing a blues feeling to a jazz improvisation.

Fig. 5. is a bass line for "Willow Weep for Me." Fig. 6 illustrates an improvised line on Fig. 5 employing "blues" devices. Transfer the melody to manuscript paper using three staves. Write or play an improvised line using Fig. 6 as a model.

Fig. 5.

I $^{+6}$ IVx / I $^{+6}$ IVx / I II / III VI Vm ♭V / IVx ♭V $^{♭5}$ / IVx IVm /

III ♭IIIx / II ♭IIx / I $^{+6}$ IVx / I $^{+6}$ IVx / I II / III VI Vm ♭V /

IVx ♭V $^{♭5}$/ IVx V $^{♭5}$ / I $^{+6}$ ♭VIx / Vm ♭V / IVm IIφ / Im Ix $^{♭5}$ /

Im IVx ♭VIIm ♭IIIx / ♭VI ♭IIx Vm Ix / IVm IIφ / Im Ix $^{♭5}$ /

Im IVx ♭VIIm ♭IIIx / ♭VI ♭IIx II ♭IIx / I $^{+6}$ IVx / I $^{+6}$ IVx / I II /

III VI Vm ♭V / IVx ♭V $^{♭5}$ / IVx V $^{♭5}$ / I $^{+6}$ / I $^{+6}$ //

Fig. 6.

SECTION IX

LESSON 62.

Patterns—Circle of Fifths

It is apparent to the student from even a casual examination of the bass lines in the previous lessons that each tune uses patterns which are common to all other tunes. These patterns occur in several designs:

1. Circle of Fifths.
2. Diatonic.
3. Chromatic.

Fig. 1 illustrates the twelve keys in the natural order of their signatures (C - no♯; no♭; G - 1♯; D - 2♯; etc.).

Fig. 1. Jazz circle.

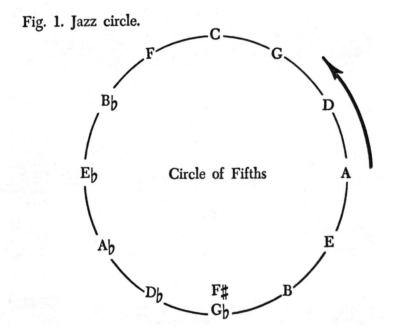

The circle can move clockwise through the sharps into the flats or counterclockwise through the flats into the sharps.

The jazz circle moves counterclockwise.

If we place a number over each letter relating to the key of C, we derive the following:

Fig. 2. Jazz circle.

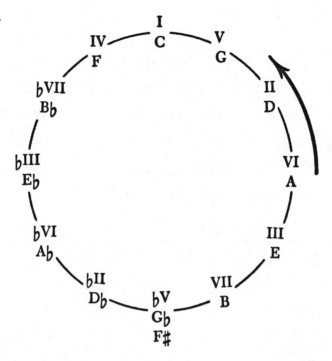

In practical terms, this means:
     V normally moves to I;
     II normally moves to V;
     VI normally moves to II;
     III normally moves to VI; etc.

The following patterns employ the circle of fifths:
     II - V - I
     III - VI - II - V - I
     IIIφ - VIx - IIφ - V - I
     VIIm - IIIx - VI - IIx - V - I
     I - IV - VIIm - III - VI - II - V - I
     ♭Vφ - VIIx - IIIφ - VIx - IIφ - V - I

These patterns should be practiced in twelve keys with both hands.

Fig. 3 is a bass line for "Pick Yourself Up," in the key of F. Note the key changes. This is an example of a tune employing the circle of fifths in a key series. Using the transposition method described in Lesson 32, transpose Fig. 3 into twelve keys. The key series in Fig. 3 is as follows: I - II - ♯II - I. Improvise on Fig. 3.

Fig. 3.

(F) II V / I IV / VII IIIx / VI IIx / V IV / III ♭IIIx /

(F) II ♭IIx / I⁺⁶ / (G) II V / I IV / VII IIIx / VI IIx /

(G) V IV / III ♭IIIx / II ♭IIx / I⁺⁶ / (A♭) I II / III VI /

(A♭) ♭VIx V / I / (F) III₂ ♭V∅$^4_3$ / III$^4_3$ VI / V IV /

(F) III ♭IIIx / II V / I IV / VII IIIx / VI IIx / V IV /

(F) III ♭IIIx / II ♭IIx / I⁺⁶ //

LESSON 63.

Patterns—Diatonic

The term diatonic refers to the normal major scale. Diatonic patterns move through the steps of the scale both ascending and descending.

Diatonic patterns usually appear in short fragments and are often combined with chromatic or circle patterns (*see* Fig. 1).

Fig. 1.

I - II - III - ♭III - II
I - VII - VI - ♭VI - Vm
II - III - IV - ♯IVx - V
IV - III - II - ♭IIx - I
IV - V - VI - ♭VIx - V
VI - V - IV - III - II - V - I

Practice these patterns in twelve keys using both hands.

Fig. 2 is a bass line for "Tea for Two," in the key of A♭. As in the previous lesson, transpose Fig. 2 into twelve keys; the key series is I - III - I.

Fig. 2.

(A♭) II III / IV $V^{\flat 5}$ / I II / III ♭IIIo / II III / IV $V^{\flat 5}$ /
(A♭) I II / III IV / (C) II III / IV $V^{\flat 5}$ / I II / III ♭IIIo /
(C) II III / IV $V^{\flat 5}$ / I IIIo / (A♭) V IV III ♭IIIx / II III /
(A♭) IV $V^{\flat 5}$ / I II / III ♭IIIo / II III / IV $V^{\flat 5}$ / IIIϕ /
(A♭) ♭IIIx / II IIIϕ / ♭VIIx VIx / ♯Io II / III IVm^{+6} /
(A♭) VI^{4}_{3} ♭IIIo / II ♭IIx / I^{+6} / I^{+6} //

TEA FOR TWO—Lyrics by Irving Caesar, Music by Vincent Youmans

LESSON 64.

Patterns—Chromatic

Chromatic patterns also appear in short fragments. Common chromatic patterns are:

II - ♭IIx - I
III - ♭IIIx - II - ♭IIx - I
I - ♯Io - II - ♯IIo - III
III - ♭IIIo - II - ♭IIM - I
♭Vϕ - IVo - III - ♭IIIo - II - ♭IIx - I

Practice these patterns in twelve keys using both hands.

Fig. 1 is a bass line for "Jeepers Creepers," in the key of B♭. Transfer the melody to manuscript paper noting key changes. Transpose to twelve keys using the following key series chart: I - IV - V - I. Improvise on Fig. 1.

Fig. 1.

(B♭) ♭Vϕ IVo / III ♭IIIo / II ♭IIx / I^{+6} VI / ♭Vϕ IVo /
(B♭) III ♭IIIo / II ♭IIx / I^{+6} VI / ♭Vϕ IVo / III ♭IIIo /
(B♭) II ♭IIx / I^{+6} VI / ♭Vϕ IVo ./ III ♭IIIo / II ♭IIx /
(B♭) I^{+6} ♯IVo / (E♭) II IVo / III ♭IIIx / II ♭IIx / I VI /
(F) II IVo / III ♭IIIx / II ♭IIx / (B♭) $V^{\sharp 3}$ V / ♭Vϕ IVo /
(B♭) III ♭IIIo / II ♭IIx / I^{+6} VI / ♭Vϕ IVo / IIIϕ ♭IIIx /
(B♭) II IVo / VI^{4}_{3} ♭IIIx / II ♭IIx / I^{+6} //

JEEPERS CREEPERS—by Johnny Mercer and Harold Warren

SECTION X

Minor Scale-tone Chords

Jazz is almost exclusively a major scale music. There are probably only five or six "authentic" (begin and end in minor) minor tunes in all jazz repertoire. However, the minor scale-tone chords are used a great deal in small fragments and are, for this reason, very important.

The jazz musician approaches the minor tonality in the same practical manner he approaches all musical problems.

The following minor scales are the frame for most "classical" music:
1. Harmonic minor — combination: 0 2 1 2 2 1 3 1 (Fig. 1).
2. Natural minor — combination: 0 2 1 2 2 1 2 2 (Fig. 2).
3. Melodic minor — ascending combination: 0 2 1 2 2 2 2 1 (Fig. 3); descending combination: 0 2 2 1 2 2 1 2 (Fig. 3).

Fig. 1.

Fig. 2.

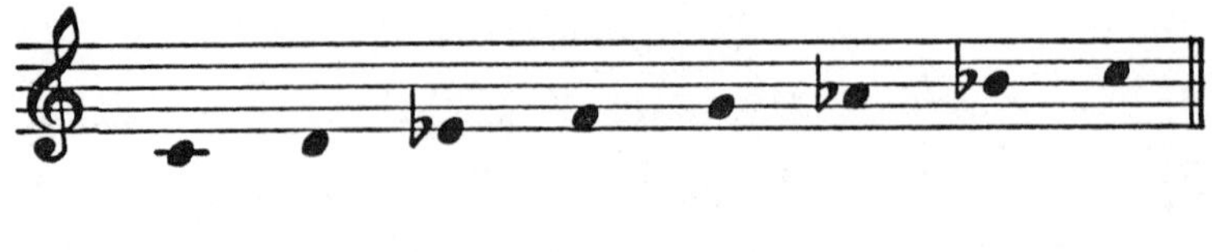

Fig. 3.

Of course, the most effective "vertical" sounds are derived from the harmonic minor. However, the use of the ♭6 in the bass line destroys familiar patterns such as   I - VI - II - V.

To avoid this, minor jazz harmony has evolved as follows:

Bass line — ascending melodic;

Inner voices — harmonic minor.

Combining these two elements, we derive the following minor scale-tone chords in C minor (*see* Fig. 4).

Fig. 4.

The minor scale-tone quality values are as follows:

POSITION	CHORD	SYMBOL
I	minor large	mL
II	half-diminished	φ
III	major augmented	M⁺
IV	minor	m
V	dominant	x
VI	half-diminished	φ
VII	diminished	o

Fig. 5 illustrates the minor scale-tone chords in G minor.

Fig. 5.

Fig. 6 illustrates the minor scale-tone chords in D minor.

Fig. 6.

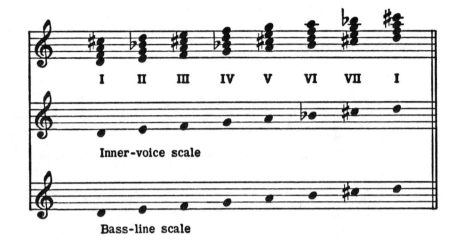

Fig. 7 illustrates the minor scale-tone chords in the remaining keys.

Fig. 7. E♭ minor scale-tone chords.

B♭ minor scale-tone chords.

F minor scale-tone chords.

A minor scale-tone chords.

E minor scale-tone chords.

B minor scale-tone chords.

A♭ minor scale-tone chords.

F♯ minor scale-tone chords.

C# minor scale-tone chords.

The minor scale-tone chords can be inverted in the same manner as the major chords. Fig. 8 illustrates the inversions of the scale-tone chords in D minor.

Fig. 8.

NOTE: The diminished chord is always in root position.

Fig. 9 is a bass line for "Yesterdays," in D minor. Transfer the melody to manuscript paper noting key change to B♭ major and the return to D minor. Since "Yesterdays" is written in half-time, the time values of each melodic tone must be doubled in order to create the necessary rhythmic framework for a jazz improvisation. Thus:

160

Fig. 9.

(d) I^{+6} VI / II $\flat$IIx / I^{+6} VI / II $\flat$IIx / I^{+6} I_2 / Im_2 /

(d) VI / IIx / ($B\flat$) VIIx$^{\sharp5}$ / IIIx / VIx / IIx / II $\flat$IIx / I VI /

(d) II / $\flat$IIx / I^{+6} VI / II $\flat$IIx / I^{+6} VI / II $\flat$IIx /

(d) I^{+6} I_2 / Im_2 / VI / IIx / ($B\flat$) VIIx$^{\sharp5}$ / IIIx / VIx / IIx /

($B\flat$) II $\flat$IIx / I VI / (d) II / $\flat$IIx / I^{+6} / I^{+6} //

DRILL: Practice the minor scale-tone chords in twelve keys using both hands.

LESSON 66.

Minor Scale-tone Arpeggios

The minor scale-tone chords involve two new qualities: I which is mL and III which is M+. The minor large chord has appeared before as a suspended minor. The major augmented has appeared as a suspended major.

Arpeggios for these chords follow the tones as they appear in the chords.

Fig. 1 is a bass line for "My Funny Valentine," in C minor. This is not an authentic minor tune since its final resolution occurs in major. This is characteristic of many tunes in the jazz repertoire. Transfer the melody to manuscript paper and play the appropriate arpeggios of the chord changes. Note the key change.

Fig. 1.

(c) I^{+6} / I_2 / Im_2 / VI / IV^6_5 Vm / IV IV_2 / II / $\flat$IIx /

(c) I^{+6} / I_2 / Im_2 / VI / ($E\flat$) IV / III $\flat$IIIx / II / $\flat$IIx /

($E\flat$) I / II / III / IV IVϕ / III $\flat$VIIx / VI $\flat$VIx Vm $\flat$V /

($E\flat$) IV II / (c) II $\flat$IIx / I^{+6} / I_2 / Im_2 / VI / IV^6_5 / II^4_3 V /

(c) Im VIIx / ($E\flat$) Vm $\flat$V / IV III / II $\flat$IIx / I^{+6} / I^{+6} //

LESSON 67.

Minor Scale-tone Scales

The minor scale-tone scales follow the rules described for the major chords. Scales for the mL and M⁺ chords appear in Lesson 48.

The following is a bass line for "Just One of Those Things," in the key of D minor. This also is not an authentic minor tune. Many "minor" tunes such as this and "My Funny Valentine" start on the VI of the final major key which is often referred to as the relative minor. It is more practical to think of it as VI.

Transfer the melody to manuscript paper noting key changes. Abandon the melody and play appropriate scales with the chord changes. Improvise on the bass lines in Lessons 65, 66 and 67.

pick-up
(d) ♭IIx // I⁺⁶ / VI / II / V / (F) Vm / Ix / ♭Vϕ / IVo /

(F) III / ♭IIIx / II / ♭IIx / I⁺⁶/ #Io / II II₂ / (d) II ♭IIx /

(d) I⁺⁶ / VI / II / V / (F) Vm / Ix / ♭Vϕ / IVo / III / ♭IIIx /

(F) II / ♭IIx / I⁺⁶ / #Io / (E♭) II / V / I / #Io / II / V /

(E♭) I⁺⁶ / Im IVx / (C) II / ♭IIx / I⁺⁶ / VI / ♭Vϕ / IVo /

(C) III / ♭IIIo / (d) IV IV₂ / II ♭IIx / I⁺⁶ / VI / II / V /

(F) Vm / Ix / IV / ♭VIIx / III / ♭IIIx / II / ♭IIx / I⁺⁶ / I⁺⁶ /

(F) I⁺⁶ / I⁺⁶ //

SECTION XI

LESSON 68.

Open Position—Axis of the Seventh

The problems of style are beyond the scope of this book. However, some primary studies in tonal organization are necessary as a preparation for future work in keyboard conception. These primary studies are derived from the major scale-tone chords and involve a simple rearrangement of the tones.

Fig. 1 illustrates the normal scale-tone chords in the key of C in what is called *closed position*.

Fig. 1.

Fig. 2 illustrates the same chords in *open position*: root and fifth in the left hand, third and seventh in the right hand. This position of the tones is called the *axis of the seventh* (seventh is top voice).

Fig. 2.

Fig. 3 illustrates the scale-tone chords of G in open position — axis of the seventh.

Fig. 3.

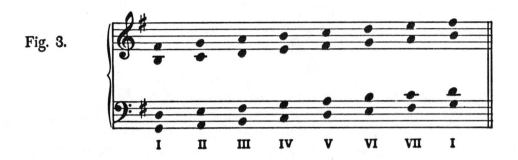

Fig. 4 illustrates the scale-tone chords of F in open position — axis of the seventh.

Fig. 4.

Fig. 5 illustrates the five *qualities* on C, open position — axis of the seventh.

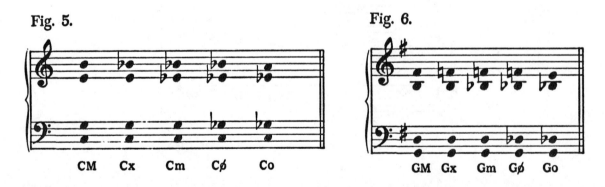

Fig. 6 illustrates the five qualities on G, open position — axis of the seventh.

Inversions, being rearranged scale-tone chords, have no third, fifth and seventh as such. However, they are treated in the same manner as normal or altered scale-tone chords. The first and third notes of the inversion are played with the left hand and the second and fourth notes of the inversion are played with the right hand. The student should remember that diminished chords cannot be inverted. Fig. 7 illustrates the inversions on the five qualities, derived from the axis of the seventh, in the key of E♭.

Fig. 7.

DRILL: Play the scale-tone seventh chords, open position, axis of the seventh in twelve keys. All five qualities on twelve tones with their inversions.

Fig. 8 is a bass line for "When Your Lover Has Gone," in the key of G. Transfer the melody to manuscript paper. In ad lib style, play the chords in open position integrating the melody in octaves. (See Fig. 9. Copyright laws prohibit exact reproduction of the melody.)

Fig. 8.

I / I / IVx / IVx / IIx♭⁵ / IIx♭⁵ / ♭VIIx / ♭VIIx / I / I VI /

IIx / ♯IIo / II / IVø / III ♭IIIx / II ♭IIx / I / I / IVx / IVx /

IIx♭⁵ / IIx♭⁵ / ♭VIIx / ♭VIIx / I / I IVm / III / ♭IIIx /

II / ♭IIM / I / I⁺⁶ //

Fig. 9.

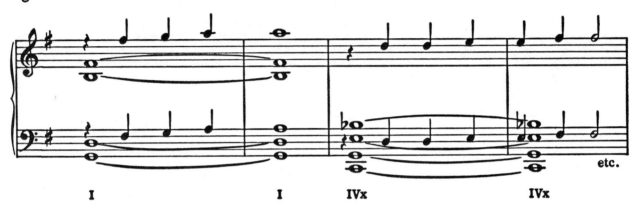

Fig. 10 is a bass line for "When Your Lover Has Gone." Play Fig. 10 integrating melody as in Fig. 9.

Fig. 10.

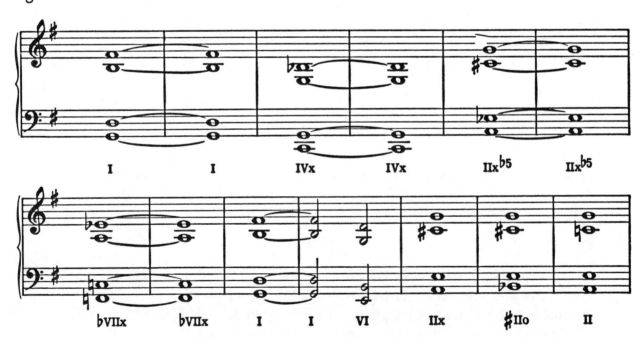

166

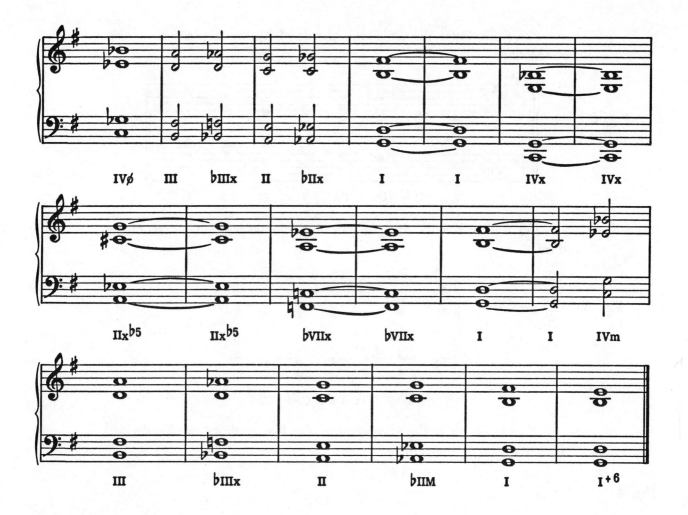

IV∅ III bIIIx II bIIx I I IVx IVx

IIx♭5 IIx♭5 bVIIx bVIIx I I IVm

III bIIIx II bIIM I I^{+6}

LESSON 69.

Open Position—Axis of the Third

Fig. 1 illustrates the scale-tone chords in B♭ in open position, axis of the third (third is top voice). The root and fifth are played with the left hand. The seventh and the third are played with the right hand.

Fig. 1.

I II III IV V VI VII I

Fig. 2 illustrates the scale-tone chords of Ab, open position — axis of the third.

Fig. 2.

Fig. 3 illustrates the five *qualities* on Db, open position — axis of the third.

Fig. 3.

Fig. 4 illustrates the inversions of the five qualities on Ab derived from the axis of the third.

Fig. 4.

Fig. 5 is a bass line for "I've Got You Under My Skin," in Eb. Transfer the melody to manuscript paper noting key changes. As in the previous lesson, play the chords in ad lib style in open position, axis of the third, integrating the melody in octaves.

168

(E♭) #Io^{pick-up} // II / ♭IIx^{♭5} / I / #Io / II / ♭IIx^{♭5} / I / VI /

(E♭) II / IVo / III / ♭IIIo / II / ♭IIx^{♭5}/ I / #Io / II / ♭IIx^{♭5}

(E♭) I / #Io / IIφ / ♭IIx^{♭5} / I / I⁺⁶ / (C) II / ♭IIx^{♭5} /

(C) I / VI // (E♭) II / ♭IIx / I / VI / II / IVo / III / ♭IIIx /

(E♭) II / IVo / III ♭IIIx / II V / ♭Vφ / IVo / III / ♭IIIo /

(E♭) II / ♭IIx^{♭5} / I VI / Vm ♭V / IV / IVo / III VI /

(E♭) IIIφ ♭IIIx / II / ♭IIx / I⁺⁶ / I⁺⁶ //

Fig. 5.

I'VE GOT YOU UNDER MY SKIN—by Cole Porter

DRILL: Play the scale-tone chords in open position, axis of the third, in twelve keys; all five qualities and their inversions on twelve tones.

NOTE: Both these chords and those illustrated in Lesson 68 are among the basic devices used by jazz pianists when "comping" (accompanying another instrument within a group).

LESSON 70.

Open Position—Mixed Axis

By combining the two axis positions, it is possible to achieve a smoother voice-leading than is possible when only a single axis is used.

Fig. 1 illustrates the circle of fifths described in Lesson 62.

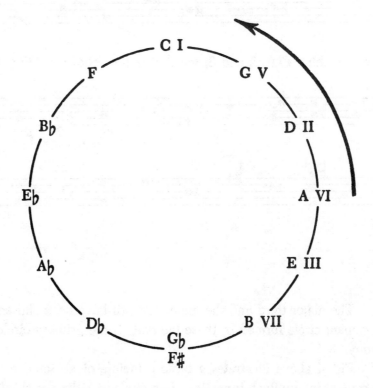

If we play a descending chromatic scale beginning on the major third with the circle described above, we derive Fig. 2 (the jazz circle, like the circle in all tonal music, moves counterclockwise).

Fig. 2.

If we play the circle a second time with a descending chromatic scale beginning on the minor seventh, we derive the following (Fig. 3):

Fig. 3.

Fig. 4.   If we combine Figs. 2 and 3, we derive the following (Fig. 4):

The major third and the minor seventh have been chosen because the dominant circle formed by these intervals is the primary circle in jazz harmony.

Fig. 4 above illustrates a basic principle of all tonal harmony which is evident in any Bach Invention: In a circle of fifths, the third becomes the seventh and the seventh becomes the third.

Fig. 5 is a bass line for "Lover Man," in the key of F. Transfer the melody to manuscript paper noting key changes. As in Lessons 68 and 69, play the chords in ad lib style in open position integrating the melody in octaves.

Numbers over the Roman numerals indicate axis to be played on each chord to insure smooth voice-leading.

172

Fig. 5.

(F) VI IIx / VI IIx / II V / II V / Ix / IVx / ♭V́Íx IÍx ♭IÍx /

(F) I IV VIIm IIIx / VI IIx / VI IIx / II V / II V / Ix / IVx /

(F) ♭V́Íx IÍx ♭IÍx / I / (G) II##7 II#7 / II ♭IÍx / I II / III II /

(F) II##7 II#7 / II ♭IÍx / I IV / VII IIIx / VI IIx / VI IIx /

(F) II V / II V / Ix / IVx / ♭V́Íx IÍx ♭IÍx / I //

Fig. 5.

LOVER MAN (Oh Where Can You Be?)—by Jimmy Davis, Roger "Ram" Ramirez, and
Jimmy Sherman

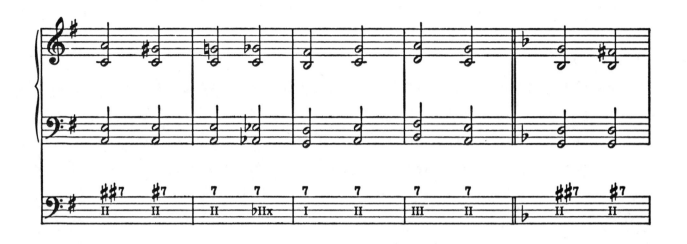

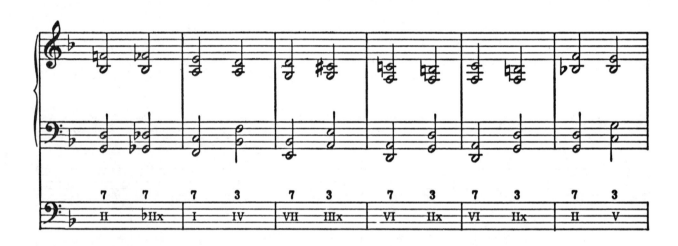

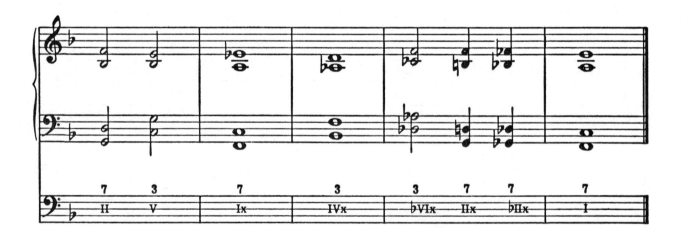

Basic Professional Piano (melodic)

We now have in our grasp sufficient material to play what might be called basic professional piano. In other words, most professional players seem able to reproduce a simple but effective sound which fulfills minimal requirements. This sound does not demand a florid technique and, above all, does not sound like sheet music. It is based on one primary factor that is used in whole or in part by every professional pianist playing today. This basic idea is open position — axis of the third and axis of the seventh. However, the use of the octave melody in Lessons 68, 69 and 70 is awkward in that the phrasing of the melodic line must be constantly interrupted in order that the chords be played at their appointed positions. This device was used only to introduce the mechanics of this type of keyboard orchestration.

The professional uses the axis technique but, instead of playing the melody in octaves, he simply adds the melody to the right hand in a single voice above the third or the seventh (*see* Fig. 1).

Fig. 1.

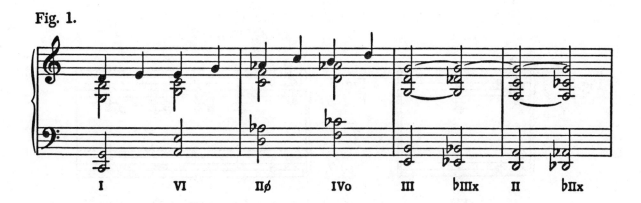

The simple rule for this procedure is as follows: Play the root and fifth in the left hand. Play the melody in the right hand, adding the nearest third and seventh immediately below the melody.

For example, in Fig. 2, the melody note is D, the chord is I in the key of C. The root (C) and fifth (G) are played in the left hand; the melody (D) is played in the right hand; the two nearest axis points below the melody are the seventh (B) and the third (E).

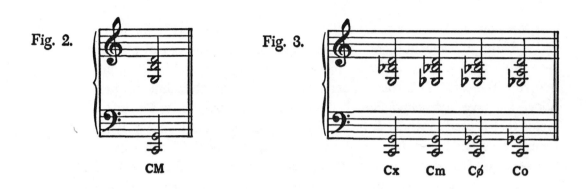

Fig. 3 illustrates the D melody note with the Cx, Cm, Cφ and Co chords. In each case, the axis formed by the D with the C chords is that of the seventh.

In Fig. 4, the melody note is G, the chord is I in the key of F. Here, the two nearest axis points below the melody are E (seventh) and A (third).

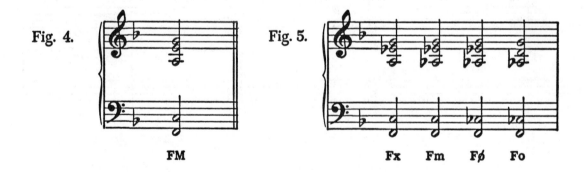

Fig. 5 illustrates the G melody note with the Fx, Fm, Fφ and Fo chords. Here the axis (top voice) is the seventh.

NOTE: When the melody note falls on the third or the seventh (see Fig. 6), double the voice an octave below in order to maintain three voices in the right hand.

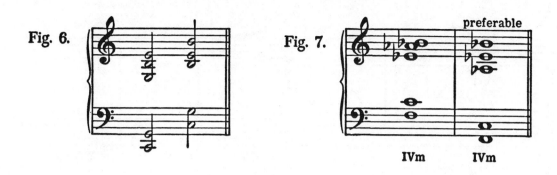

Generally, the axis of the seventh is the stronger and should be used whenever it is physically possible. In Fig. 7, the second voicing is preferable to the first for harmonic depth. However, this is a corollary of the basic rule of the third and the seventh immediately below.

Fig. 8 illustrates the application of this technique to the melody in Lesson 7, Fig. 1.

Fig. 8.

179

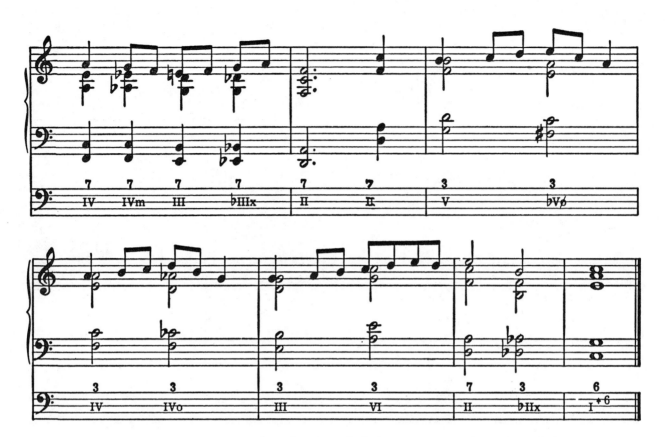

Fig. 10 is a bass line for "Tenderly," in D. Transfer the melody to manuscript paper. "Tenderly" appears as a waltz in the sheet music version and must be converted to 4/4 time by the simple device of adding one beat to the first note of each bar, as in Fig. 9.

Fig. 9.

The numbers over the symbols in Fig. 10 indicate the axis in each case which is determined by the melody note position.

Fig. 10.

TENDERLY—Lyrics by Jack Lawrence, Music by Walter Gross

LESSON 72.

Basic Professional Piano (improvised)

Jazz piano until 1940 was dominated by the concept of swing bass which was evolved from the early ragtime period. The four masters of swing bass piano were Earl Hines, Fats Waller, Teddy Wilson and Art Tatum.

One of Tatum's most spectacular devices in the left hand was a circle of fifths pattern of alternating full tenths and sevenths (*see* Fig. 1).

Fig. 1.

This was not a swing-bass design as such although it did give the feeling of the quarter-note pulse basic to swing-bass piano.

The student will notice that Fig. 1 is almost identical with Fig. 4, Lesson 70, except that the bass design has been inverted. The student will also notice that he probably is unable to play many of the tenths (D♭ involves the widest stretch).

After 1940 the problem facing the jazz pianist was to evolve a left hand style that would no longer contain the rigid symmetry of swing bass, but at the same time would fulfill basic harmonic requirements. In other words, the rhythmic responsibility of jazz piano was taken from the left hand and placed in the right.

Although many pianists were involved in this revolutionary step, the master figure is Earl "Bud" Powell. Powell's solution to this problem was magnificently simple (Fig. 2). This is Fig. 2 of Lesson 70 reduced to one hand.

These thirds (fingering 2-1) and sevenths (fingering 5-1) are usually referred to as "shells"—the term refers to the more common seventh shell employment of the outer elements of the chord.

182

Fig. 2.

If we compare the first two steps of the series in Figs. 1 and 2, we find the following (Fig. 3):

Fig. 3.

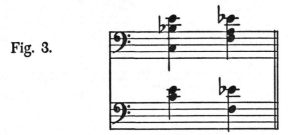

In the top stave of Fig. 3, both chords are dominant since both contain a major third and a minor seventh (whether the omitted fifth were perfect, diminished or augmented, the chord would remain dominant). In the bottom stave of Fig. 3, the shell C-E could represent the following chord fragments:

SHELL	QUALITY FRAGMENT
C - E	CM (C - E - G - B)
C - E	Cx (C E G Bb)

Again, in the bottom stave of Fig. 3, the interval F-Eb could represent the following chord fragments:

SHELL	QUALITY FRAGMENT
F - Eb	Fx (F - A - C - Eb)
F - Eb	Fm (F - Ab - C - Eb)
F - Eb	Fo (F - Ab - Cb - Eb)

This means that the series in Fig. 2 only "implies" certain qualities—the missing tones (3rd, 5th or 7th) must appear in the right hand improvisation (Fig. 4).

Fig. 4.

These left hand shells are indicated by a point system as follows:

(Key of F) III⁷ - VIx³ - II⁷ - V³ - I⁷ which reads:

III — point of seven
VIx — point of three
II — point of seven
V — point of three
I — point of seven

(*See* Fig. 5.)

Fig. 5.

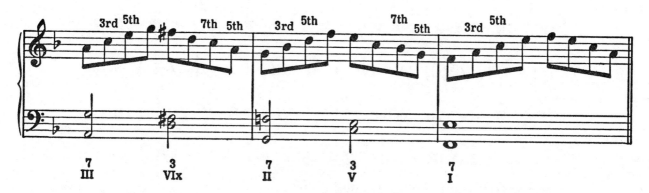

Inversions are indicated by playing the outside voices of the particular inversion and are always played at the point of six (in all inversions the distance between the top voice is either a major or minor sixth — so too with +6) (Fig. 6).

Fig. 6.

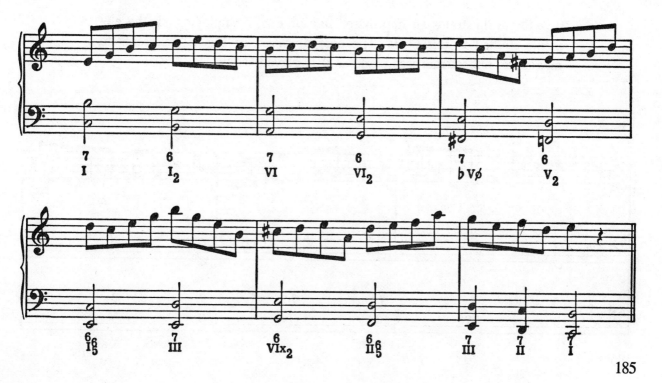

Fig. 7 is a bass line for "Gone with the Wind," in E♭. Transfer the melody to manuscript paper noting key changes. Numbers over Roman numerals indicate interval point of chord in left hand.

Fig. 7. "Gone with the Wind"

(E♭) $\overset{7}{II}$ $\overset{7}{IV}o$ / $\overset{7}{III}$ $\overset{3}{VI}x$ / $\overset{7}{II}$ $\overset{7}{V}$ / $\overset{7}{I}$ $\overset{6}{I_2}$ / (G) $b\overset{7}{V}\phi$ $\overset{7}{IV}o$ / $\overset{7}{III}$ $\overset{3}{VI}x$ /

(G) $\overset{7}{II}$ $\overset{3}{V}$ / $\overset{7}{I}$ $\overset{6}{I}\overset{+}{}{}^6$ / (E♭) $\overset{7}{III}$ / $b\overset{7}{III}o$ / $\overset{7}{II}$ / $\overset{3}{V}$ / $\overset{7}{I}$ $\overset{7}{VII}x$ /

(E♭) $\overset{7}{III}\phi$ $\overset{3}{VI}x$ / $\overset{7}{II}$ / $\overset{3}{V}$ / $b\overset{7}{V}\phi$ $\overset{7}{IV}o$ / $\overset{7}{III}$ $b\overset{7}{III}x$ / $\overset{7}{II}$ $b\overset{7}{II}x$ /

(E♭) $\overset{7}{I}$ $\overset{6}{I_2}$ / (G) $b\overset{7}{V}\phi$ $\overset{7}{IV}o$ / $\overset{7}{III}$ $b\overset{7}{III}x$ / $\overset{7}{II}$ $b\overset{7}{II}x$ / $\overset{7}{I}$ $\overset{7}{VII}o$ /

(E♭) $\overset{7}{II}$ $\overset{6}{II_2}$ $\overset{7}{VII}$ $b\overset{7}{VII}x$ / $\overset{\sharp\sharp7}{VI}$ $\overset{7}{VI}$ / $\overset{7}{II}$ $\overset{3}{V}$ / $\overset{7}{III}$ $\overset{3}{VI}x$ /

(E♭) $II\overset{\sharp\sharp\sharp7}{}$ $II\overset{\sharp7}{}$ / $\overset{7}{II}$ $b\overset{7}{II}x$ / $\overset{7}{I}$ / $\overset{6}{I}\overset{+}{}{}^6$ //

Fig. 8 illustrates an improvised line of Fig. 7 employing all the elements studied in this book. The over-all sound of Fig. 8 represents in microcosm mainstream jazz piano as it is played today.

Fig. 8.

189

DRILL: Write or play an improvisation on Fig. 7. Apply this style technique to previous assignments in the book using the following simple rules:

1. In diatonic progressions (Fig. 9), use sevenths only.

Fig. 9

2. In chromatic progressions (Fig. 10), use sevenths only.

Fig. 10.

3. In circles of fifths progressions (Fig. 11), use point of seven on all major, minor, half-diminished and diminished chords; on all dominant chords, use point of three. Dominants in Rules 1 and 2 always take point of seven. Alternate consecutive dominants with three and seven when in circle of fifths.

Fig. 11 illustrates the basic circle of fifths series from the twelve positions. All thirds to be fingered 2-1; all sevenths 5-1.

In a schematic such as Fig. 11, all accidentals terminate where they originally appeared.

The student is strongly advised to study and memorize Fig. 11 in order to create the automatic facility necessary to jazz performing.

Fig. 11.

191

Fig. 12 illustrates a stylized bass line on Fig. 2 in Lesson 60.

Fig. 12.

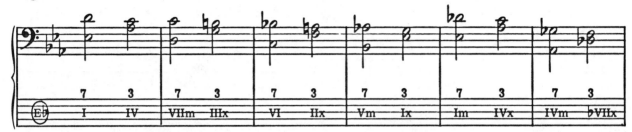

In general, the fifth finger of the left hand should appear in the second octave below middle C, which means that the hand is shifted down one octave from the scale-tone chord position (*see* Fig. 13).

Fig. 13.

192

SECTION XII

LESSON 73.

Standard Procedure

The following rules can be helpful in tracing the necessary steps toward a professional jazz performance.

1. Explore melody and chords in several keys.
   (The following steps refer to written key.)
2. Explore arpeggios for each chord.
3. Explore scales for each chord.
4. Memorize melody and chords.
5. Memorize chords alone — no melody.

In the beginning the student may not be able to accomplish steps 4 and 5; if so, they should be skipped. However, at some later time, these steps should be learned in their natural order.

The following rules should be accompanied by a quarter-note foot beat — abandon the melody:

6. Play chords in the left hand, eighth-note arpeggios in the right hand.
7. Play chords in the left hand, eighth-note scales in the right hand.
8. Play chords in the left hand, eighth-note triplet arpeggios in the right hand.
9. Play chords in the left hand, eighth-note triplet scales in the right hand.
10. Play chords in the left hand, sixteenth-note arpeggios in the right hand.
11. Play chords in the left hand, sixteenth-note scales in the right hand.
12. Play chords in the left hand, apply rhythm combinations to arpeggios. (Lesson 38)
13. Play chords in the left hand, apply rhythm combinations to scales. (Lesson 52)
14. Play chords in the left hand, apply rhythmic composite to arpeggios. (Lessons 39, 40)
15. Play chords in the left hand, apply rhythmic composite to scales. (Lessons 53, 54)
16. Play chords in the left hand, combine previous elements into an improvisation.
17. Stylize left hand as in Lesson 72.
18. Do *not* use the sostenuto or "loud" pedal when improvising.

Ear Training

The problem of developing the ear for what is called prehearing is of major importance in performing jazz. It goes without saying that the hearing demands in jazz are extremely high and no effort should be spared in the development of the ear. The following outline indicates the hearing levels which occur simultaneously in the performance of a mature jazz musician:

_____ Improvisation
_____ Melody
_____ Lyric
_____ Chord progression
_____ Pulse or beat

To hear these five levels simultaneously is a basic prerequisite for superior jazz playing.

The following rules can be of great value in building a secure relationship between the ear, the eye and the hand.

1. Play any scale. Sing any tone of the scale and check at the keyboard.
2. Strike any tone on the keyboard and sing any of the remaining eleven tones.
3. Play any tone and sing the third, fifth and seventh of the five qualities.
4. Play and sing the scale-tone chords in twelve keys.
5. Play any scale and sing the various altered chords on each tone.
6. Play any scale and sing the various chromatic chords on each tone.
7. Play any scale and sing the various altered chromatic chords on each tone.
8. Repeat the previous steps with inversions.
9. Play the bass notes (omit the 3rd, 5th and 7th) in a two-part form and sing the melody.
10. Repeat step 9 and sing the bass line.
11. Repeat step 9 and sing the qualities of the bass line.
12. Use tenor saxophone (closest instrument to human voice) recordings to sing the saxophone "line" simultaneously with the recording.
13. Identify bass lines on recordings. Indicate bass lines in Roman numerals.
14. Play the fifteen two-part Inventions of J. S. Bach — first singing the right hand voice, then the left hand voice.

LESSON 75.

Memorization

To say that memorization is important to the playing of jazz is equivalent to saying that a knowledge of harmony and rhythm is important to the playing of jazz.

Memorizing the elements that go to make up an improvisation is concentrated in one factor — the procession of the chords in their rhythmic frame.

This chord procession includes all the elements described in the previous chapter on Ear Training. Of course, the problems of memory and hearing are closely related, although memory can operate on three levels: (1) Mental; (2) Muscular; (3) Auditory.

Method 1 (mental) is the least preferred and involves thinking of the Roman numerals comprising a bass line (I, VI, IIϕ, V, etc.).

Method 2 (muscular) involves automatic playing (memorized hand positions) which can be found in all professional playing, particularly in the classical field. In topflight jazz piano, automatic playing should be at a minimum in order to give the performer the highest degree of spontaneous rhythmic and tonal freedom. However, the muscular method can be helpful as a starting point for the student. This involves learning the various hand positions of the chords until they can be played without hesitation. When applying the outline of procedure in Lesson 73, the student will find that mastering step 4 will not necessarily mean the same for step 5. The hands will not be able to function independently in the beginning, although hand independence must eventually be achieved for good jazz playing.

Method 3 (prehearing) means a memorized hearing — heard in anticipation of the moment of playing. This is the ideal we all seek and is the reason why fine jazz playing is a challenge both to play and appreciate.

Apply the rules of procedure to all the bass lines in this book starting on whatever practical level necessary for the student.

LESSON 76.

Sheet Music Conversion

The problem in converting sheet music is one of simplification; sheet music is much too complicated to provide a simple harmonic structure for improvisation. However, sheet music is the only practical means of determining the intention of a composer. Unfortunately the aspect of most importance to the improviser — the bass line — is of comparatively minor importance to the composer.

The following steps are suggested as a means of isolating the fabric of a tune from the melody and orchestration of the sheet music.

1. Convert guitar symbols to Roman numerals. Guitar symbols appear in letters; these letters must be given a numerical position in the key. The following table on C indicates the values of the letters and their conversion. All letters will function in the same manner.

C Major:	C
	C Maj.
	C Maj. 9
	C^6
C Dominant:	C^7
	C^9
	C^{13}
	C+
C Dominant $^{\sharp 3}$:	C^7 susp. 4
C Dominant $^{\flat 5}$:	C^7+^{11}
	C+^{11}
C Minor:	Cm^7
	Cm^9
	C min.^{7}
C Half-diminished:	Cm^{-5}
	Cm$^{\flat 5}$
	E$^\flat$m^{6} *
C Diminished:	C dim.
	Co

RULE: *On all m^6 symbols, build a half-diminished chord a minor third below.*

2. Convert notation in bass and treble clefs to Roman numerals. In many cases this step can be extremely difficult; however, if the student starts with the lowest note in the bass and searches out the third, fifth and seventh, the quality of the chord should emerge. If one or more of these tones cannot be found there is a fairly clear indication of the presence of an inversion.

---

*E♭m6 is the first inversion of a C∅ chord which should be played in root position.

3. Compare the two results (letters and notation) for the best solution. This step involves the problem of removing many of the faults common to most sheet music:

(a) Unprepared dominant chords;
(b) incomplete patterns;
(c) interrupted patterns;
(d) key changes not indicated;
(e) additional chords for melodic adjustment;
(f) misspelled inversions.

The solutions are as follows:

1. When a dominant chord appears on the first beat of a bar and is held through four beats, prepare the dominant by playing a minor or half-diminished chord a perfect fifth above for the first two beats.

2. If a chord series such as I / II V / appears in sheet music, this is an incomplete pattern. It should be I VI / II V /. If III VI / V / appears, this too is an incomplete pattern. It should read III VI / II V /.

3. Interrupted patterns:

Sheet music:	Pattern:
III ♭IIIx / II V / I	III ♭IIIx / II ♭IIx / I
III VI / II ♭IIx / I	III VI / II V / I
VI VI + ⁶ / VII IIIx / VI	VI ♭Vφ / VII IIIx / VI

4. Key changes: The presence of a major chord on other than I or IV is a clear indication of a new key. If, in converting to Roman numerals, the student finds, for example, VM, II Maj. ⁶, VIM, an immediate adjustment should be made in the signature no matter how fragmentary.

5. Many sheet music bars contain three or more chords: one or two for he basic harmony and the remaining chord or chords to cover isolated melody tones which clutter the frame for an improvisation. Omit this "cover" chord.

6. Often, an inversion will appear in the notation but is spelled in the guitar symbol as a root position chord. In cases of this sort, the notation should be followed indicating the inversion position.

In concluding this lesson, the following rules are well to keep in mind:
The major chord can move anywhere.
The dominant, minor and half-diminished chords usually move down a P5 or down a m2.
The diminished chord moves up a m2 or moves down a m2.
The conversion of 3/4 time to 4/4 time is discussed in Lesson 71.

Touch—Technique

The technical demands of modern jazz playing are in many ways comparable to those required by serious music. On some jazz instruments (notably the trumpet), levels of virtuosity have often exceeded those obtaining in the concert field.

In jazz piano, Teddy Wilson and Art Tatum established the modern levels of virtuosity although their styles utilized a great deal of legato playing which has in recent years undergone vital changes.

The major figure after Wilson and Tatum is Bud Powell who, despite his revolutionary contribution to modern jazz piano (abandonment of swing bass, etc.), retained much of the finger legato playing of the earlier period. George Shearing in general continued the legato sound with an emphasis on block chords skillfully pedalled to resemble the sound of a saxophone section. Shearing's "single line" was classically conceived along the lines of a Mozart rondo.

Along with the virtuoso Powell school, there appeared the beginnings of a primitive school of pianism led by Thelonius Monk. This style remained in a relatively undeveloped stage until 1951 and the appearance of Horace Silver, who founded the modern articulation approach to jazz piano. This was a revolutionary movement away from the finger legato and toward what might be described as a "wrist" legato. This means the use of a quick wrist stroke on practically every note which is cushioned and connected by the finger clinging to the key. On fast sixteenth- and thirty-second note passages, this wrist stroke is abandoned in favor of the finger, but the essential eighth-note strokes nearly all start at the wrist. This is an attempt of the pianist to simulate the hard, sharp attack of the various jazz horns.

In the last seven years this style of articulation has become the vernacular sound of modern jazz piano. Oscar Peterson has furthered the articulation style by enhancing it with a virtuoso technique reminiscent of Art Tatum's. There is little of the classical legato in Peterson, who is undoubtedly the outstanding jazz pianist today.

Hampton Hawes has effected a fusion of the Powell architecture and Silver's touch. Hawes has brought the Charlie Parker "line" concept to the keyboard with a definite emphasis upon the articulated stroke.

This wrist stroke is *not* a staccato or half-staccato. Classically trained pianists immediately apply a staccato technique to jazz playing with disastrous results. In classical terms, the stroke is more related to a marcato attack, but never a staccato.

General knowledge and playing experience with the literature of the keyboard are essential to jazz performing, although some composers are of more value than others.

Bach, Mozart, Chopin, Brahms and Debussy are the major influences prevalent in jazz piano, although familiarity with all composers of all periods can nourish the student in his work.

Jazz hornmen are an important influence on all jazz pianists, with emphasis on the tenor and alto saxophone.

Hanon studies in twelve keys are valuable in building key facility and the diatonic feeling of jazz harmony.

In conclusion, a jazz musician can be only as good as his degree of exposure to all music regardless of the instrument or the period and, of course, as his degree of mastery of his instrument.

Recordings

Unlike the literature of classical music, jazz literature does not and cannot by its very nature appear as written or notated music. Recordings are the only permanent document of jazz literature and the responsibility of becoming familiar with this literature rests heavily upon the student.

It is important for the serious jazz student to study the basic discography of jazz from 1925 to the present day. This study should be approached on two levels — general, and specific instrument.

Study in the first category should be sufficient to identify general stylistic features of each period with a knowledge of the major figures (regardless of instrument) of each period.

Study in the second category should have reference to the specific instrument chosen by the student. Here, the research should be more intense, with serious study of each period, its stylistic patterns, the compositions played, the techniques employed, etc.

The following outline indicates some of the major figures on each of the important jazz instruments:

Arranger:	Bands:
Fletcher Henderson	Fletcher Henderson
Duke Ellington	Benny Goodman
Don Redman	Duke Ellington
Sy Oliver	Jimmie Lunceford
Gerry Mulligan	Count Basie
Bill Holman	Woody Herman
Nelson Riddle	Gerry Mulligan Tentet
	Stan Kenton

Bass:
  Pops Foster
  Jimmy Blanton
  Oscar Pettiford
  Ray Brown
  Charles Mingus

Clarinet:
  Johnny Dodds
  Pee Wee Russell
  Artie Shaw
  Benny Goodman
  Stan Hasselgard

Drums:
  Baby Dodds
  Chick Webb
  Gene Krupa
  Kenny Clarke
  Jo Jones
  Max Roach

Guitar:
  Eddie Lang
  George van Epps
  Charlie Christian
  Django Reinhardt
  Tal Farlow
  Joe Pass

Piano:
  Jelly Roll Morton
  Earl "Fatha" Hines
  Fats Waller
  Teddy Wilson
  Art Tatum
  Earl "Bud" Powell
  George Shearing
  Horace Silver
  Oscar Peterson
  Hampton Hawes
  Wynton Kelly
  Herbie Hancock
  McCoy Tyner
  Bill Evans

Alto Saxophone:
  Benny Carter
  Johnny Hodges
  Charlie Parker
  Lee Konitz

Tenor Saxophone:
  Bud Freeman
  Coleman Hawkins
  Lester Young
  Stan Getz
  John Coltrane

Miscellaneous Instruments:
  Milt Jackson—vibraphone
  Jean (Toots) Thielemans—harmonica
  Serge Chaloff—baritone saxophone
  Jimmy Smith—organ
  Red Norvo—xylophone

Trumpet:
  Buddy Bolden
  Louis Armstrong
  Bix Beiderbecke
  Roy Eldridge
  Bunny Berigan
  Dizzy Gillespie
  Miles Davis
  Chet Baker
  Clifford Brown

Trombone:
  Kid Ory
  Jack Teagarden
  Tommy Dorsey
  J.J. Johnson

Vocalists:
  Louis Armstrong
  Bessie Smith
  Jack Teagarden
  Bing Crosby
  Joe Turner
  Billie Holiday
  Eddie Jefferson
  Frank Sinatra
  Ella Fitzgerald
  Anita O'Day
  Four Freshmen
  Hi-Lo's
  Lambert-Hendricks-Ross

This list is by no means exhaustive. It is a general guide to the vast jazz literature.

It is important to remember that many of the most important advances have occurred on the trumpet and saxophone and were later transposed to other instruments; i.e., Armstrong to Hines, Parker to Powell. The point is that the "lines of influence" in serious music are fairly direct; in jazz, these lines crisscross in many ways from instrument to instrument and from period to period. Full knowledge of these transitions is essential to the development of a thorough background.

The following is a brief chronology of the history of jazz piano.

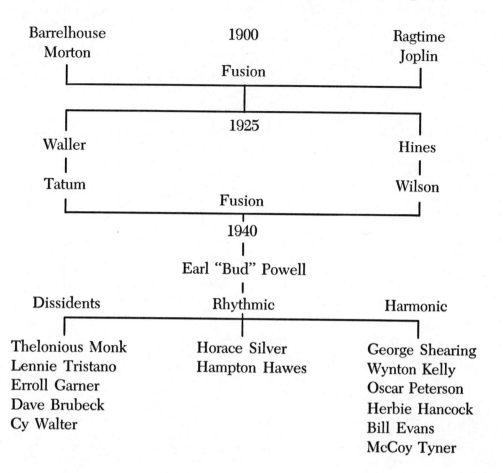

For Further Study

In this section, a number of additional figured bass lines are provided to enable the student to expand his knowledge of the preceding lessons. Follow the previously suggested procedure of writing the tune out on two or three staves, depending on which lesson is being expanded.

The song "Carolina Shout" is included here as a lesson in the style of Thomas "Fats" Waller. It is, in the opinion of the author, an ideal example of Waller's stylistic contributions.

Dolphin Dance

The following is a bass line for "Dolphin Dance" in E♭. Note key changes.

(E♭) I / Ix$^{\sharp 3}$ / I / VIIx ♭VIIx / VI VI$_2$ / IV$^{♭5}$ / VI VI$_2$ //

(G) II ♭IIx / I // (E♭) IVm IVm$_2$ II / V ♯Vo / VI / VI$_2$ //

(G) II / ♭IIx / I / Ix$^{\sharp 3}$ / Ix$^{\sharp\sharp 3}_{\text{omit 5}}$ / Ix$^{\sharp 3}$ Ix / ♭VIIx$^{\sharp 3}$ / ♭VIIx$^{\sharp\sharp 3}_{\text{omit 5}}$ /

(G) ♭VIIx$^{\sharp 3}$ / VI IIx / ♭VIx / V / III / VIx Vϕ / ♭Vm / VIIx /

(G) VIx$^{\sharp 3}$ / IV$^{6}_{5}$ / VIx$^{\sharp 3}$ / IV$^{6}_{5}$ //

DOLPHIN DANCE—by Herbie Hancock
  Courtesy of Hancock Music Co.
  Used by permission.

Invitation

The following is a bass line for "Invitation." This tune presents a unique problem due to the absence of major chords (the normal cadence chord) with the exception of the final chord. Note key changes.

(C)   II$^{\sharp\sharp7}$ / II$^{\sharp7}$ / II / V / II / V / Vm / Ix // (E♭) II$^{\sharp\sharp7}$ / II$^{\sharp7}$ /

(E♭) II / V / II / V / Vm / Ix // (D♭) II / V // (B) II$^{\sharp\sharp7}$ / II$^{\sharp7}$ /

(B)   II / V // (A) II$^{\sharp\sharp7}$ / II$^{\sharp7}$ / II / V // (C) VI / VI$_2$ / IVx$^{♭5}$ /

(C)   IVx$^{♭5}$ / IIIx$^{\sharp5}$ / ♭IIIx / II$^{\sharp\sharp7}$ / II$^{\sharp7}$ / II / V / II / V / Vm / Ix //

(E♭) II / II$_2$ / ♭VIIM$^{♭5}$ / ♭VIIM$^{♭5}$ / IIø / V$^{\sharp5}$ / Im$_L$ / Im$_L$ //

West Coast Blues

The following are a head chart and a blowing chart for "West Coast Blues" in B♭. Note 3/4 time signature.

HEAD CHART

$\frac{3}{4}$ Ix / ⁒ / ♭VIIx / ⁒ / Ix / ⁒ / ♭II / ♭II ♭VIx / IVx / ⁒ / ⁒ / ⁒ /

$\frac{3}{4}$ Ix / ⁒ / ⁒ / ⁒ / V / ⁒ / IVx / ⁒ / Ix / ♭IIIx / ♭VIM / ♭IIx //

$\frac{3}{4}$ Ix / ⁒ / ♭VIIx / ⁒ / Ix / ⁒ / ♭II / ♭II ♭VIx / IVx / ⁒ / ⁒ / ⁒ /

$\frac{3}{4}$ Ix / ⁒ / ⁒ / ⁒ / V / ⁒ / IVx / ⁒ / Ix / ♭IIIx / ♭VIM / ♭IIx //

BLOWING CHART

$\frac{3}{4}$ Ix / ⁒ / ♭VIIx / ⁒ / Ix / ⁒ / ♭II / ♭VIx / IVx / ⁒ / IVm / ♭VIIx /

$\frac{3}{4}$ III / VIx / ♭III / ♭VIx / II / III / IV / V / Ix / ♭IIIx /

$\frac{3}{4}$♭VIM / ♭IIx //

The Summer Knows

The following is a bass line for "The Summer Knows" in (f) minor. Note key changes.

pick-up
(f) $\flat$IIx // I^{+6} / I$_2$ / Im$_2$ / VI / IV / IV$_2$$^{\sharp 7}$ / IV$_2$ / II //

(F)   V$^{\sharp 3}$ V / I / IIϕ_2 / I / Vm Ix$^{\sharp 3}$ / IV // (A) IIϕ V / I V / I //

(A$\flat$) V / I V / I // (G) V / II$_2$ I // (F) IIϕ $\flat$IIx / I / IIϕ_2 / I /

(F)   IIϕ_2 // (f) Im / IV / I^{+6} / I^{+6} //

Time After Time

The following is a bass line for "Time After Time" in B$\flat$.

I VI / II V$^{\sharp 3}$ / III VI / II V$^{\sharp 3}$ / I / IV / VIIm / IIIx / VI VI$_2$ /

$\flat$Vϕ VIIx / III$^{\sharp\sharp 7}$ III$^{\sharp 7}$ / IIIϕ VIx / II$^{\sharp\sharp 7}$ II$^{\sharp 7}$ / II $\flat$VIx / V$^{\sharp 3}$ / V /

I VI / II V$^{\sharp 3}$ / III VI / II V$^{\sharp 3}$ / Í VÍ $\flat$VÍo / Vm $\flat$V / IV / $\flat$VIIx /

I Ix$_2$ / IIx$^{\overset{4}{3}}$ II$\phi^{\overset{4}{3}}$ / VI$_2$ $\flat$V / IVm $\flat$VIIx / III $\flat$IIIo / II $\flat$IIx / I^{+6} /

I^{+6} //

For All We Know

The following is a bass line for "For All We Know" in the key of F.

pick-up
$\flat$IIx // I VI / IIx$^{\flat 5}$ / V / II $\flat$IIx / I II / IIIϕ $\flat$IIIx / II$^{\sharp\sharp 7}$ II$^{\sharp 7}$ /

II $\sharp$IIo / III / $\flat$IIIo / II II$_2$ / VIIm $\flat$VIIx / VI$^{\sharp\sharp 7}$ VI$^{\sharp 3}$ / VI $\flat$IIIo /

II / V$^{\sharp 3}$ / I VI / IIx$^{\flat 5}$ / V / II $\flat$IIx / I II   IIIϕ $\flat$IIIx / II$^{\sharp\sharp 7}$ II$^{\sharp 7}$ /

II $\sharp$IIo / III VI / $\flat$Vm VIIx / IIIx $\flat$VIIx$^{\flat 5}$ / VIx$^{\sharp 3}$ VIx / II $\flat$VIx$^{\flat 5}$ /

V$^{\sharp 3}$ V / I^{+6} / I^{+6} //

The Preacher

The following is a figured bass for "The Preacher" in F.

$V^{\sharp 3}$ // I $\flat$VIo / Vm $\flat$V / IVx $\flat$VIIx / I $V^{\sharp 3}$ /

pick-up
$\bar{I}$ $\bar{IV}$ $V\bar{I}Im$ $I\bar{I}Ix$ / $VI^{\sharp\sharp 7}$ $VI^{\sharp 7}$ / VI IIx / II $V^{\sharp 3}$ / I $\flat$VIo / Vm Ix /

Im IVx / VIIm IIIx / IV^{+6} $\sharp$IVo / VI_2 VI / II $V^{\sharp 3}$ / I^{+6} $V^{\sharp 3}$ /

I^{+6} $V^{\sharp 3}$ // I $\flat$VIo / Vm $\flat$V / IVx $\flat$VIIx / I $V^{\sharp 3}$ / $\bar{I}$ $\bar{IV}$ $V\bar{I}Im$ $I\bar{I}Ix$ /

$VI^{\sharp\sharp 7}$ $VI^{\sharp 7}$ / VI IIx / II $V^{\sharp 3}$ / I $\flat$VIo / Vm Ix / Im IVx / VIIm IIIx /

IV^{+6} $\sharp$IVo / VI_2 VI / II $V^{\sharp 3}$ / I^{+6} $V^{\sharp 3}$ / I^{+6} //

Desifinado

The following is a figured bass for "Desifinado." Note key changes.

(F) I / ℅ / $IIx^{\flat 5}$ / ℅ / II / V / IIIϕ / VIx / II II_2 //

(D) IIϕ V / I / Ix // (F) VIϕ / IIx / $\flat$IIM / ℅ / I / ℅ / $IIx^{\flat 5}$ /

(F) ℅ / II / V / IIIϕ / VIx / II III / IVm $\flat$VIIx / I VI //

(A) IIϕ $\flat$IIx / I / VI / II / V / III   VI / II / V / I / VI / II / V //

(F) VIIm / $IIIx^{\flat 5}$ / VI / IIx / II / $\flat$IIIx / IIx / $\flat$IIx / I / ℅ /

(F) $IIx^{\flat 5}$ / ℅ / II / V / IIIϕ / VIx / II III / IVm $\flat$VIIx / I VI /

(F) IIx / $\flat$Vϕ / IVm / $IIIx^{\sharp 5}$ / $\flat$IIIx / IIx / $\flat$IIM / I / I^{+6} //

Our Love Is Here to Stay

The following is a bass line for "Our Love Is Here to Stay" in the key of F.

pick-up

VI // IIx^{b5} / II V$^{\sharp3}$ / I^{+6} II / III VI / IIx^{b5} / II II$_2$ / $\flat$VIIx VIx /

IIx $\sharp$IIo / III VIx / II V / I IV / VII IIIx / VI$^{\sharp\sharp7}$ VI$^{\sharp7}$ / VI IIx /

II $\flat$VIx / V VI / IIx^{b5} / II V$^{\sharp3}$ / I^{+6} II / III VI / IIx^{b5} / II II$_2$ /

$\flat$VIIx VIx / IIx $\sharp$IIo / III VIx / II V / Vm Ix / IV^{+6} $\sharp$IVo / VI$_2$ VI /

II V$^{\sharp3}$ / I^{+6} / I^{+6} //

OUR LOVE IS HERE TO STAY—by George and Ira Gershwin
    © 1938 by Chappell & Co., Inc. © renewed.
    International copyright secured. All rights reserved.
    Used by permission.

Here's That Rainy Day

The following is a bass line for "Here's That Rainy Day" in B$\flat$. Note key changes.

(B$\flat$) I VIIx$^{\sharp5}$ // (G$\flat$) III$_2$ $\flat$IIx / I / IV //

(B$\flat$) II III / IV V / I VI / Vm $\flat$V //

(D$\flat$) II$^{\sharp\sharp7}$ II$^{\sharp7}$ / II $\flat$IIx / I $\flat$V / I$\acute{\text{V}}$ I$\acute{\text{V}}_2$ I$\acute{\text{I}}$ I$\acute{\text{I}}_2$ //

(B$\flat$) II$^{\sharp\sharp7}$ II$^{\sharp7}$ / II V / $\flat$VIIx VIx / $\flat$VIx V / I VIIx$^{\sharp5}$ //

(G$\flat$) III$_2$ $\flat$IIx / I / IV //

(B$\flat$) II III / IV V / Ix / Vm $\flat$V / IV /

(B$\flat$) VII$^4_3$ IVo / III VI / IIx / II III / IV V / I^{+6} / I^{+6} //

HERE'S THAT RAINY DAY—by Burke and Van Heusen
    © 1953 by Burke & Van Heusen, Inc. © assigned to Bourne Co. & Dorsey Bros.
    Music, Inc. © renewed.
    Used by permission.

The Girl from Ipanema

The following is a bass line for "The Girl from Ipanema" in F. Note key changes.

(F)   I / I / IIx^{b5} / IIx^{b5} / II / IVϕ / III bIIIx / II bIIx / I / I / IIx^{b5} /

(F)   IIx^{b5} / II / bIIx / I / I // (F♯) I / I / IVx / IVx / Im / Im //

(F)   VIx / VIx / II / II / bVIIx / bVIIx / III / VIx^{b5} / II / V^{b5} /

(F)   I / I / IIx^{b5} / IIx^{b5} / II / bIIx / I / bIIx / I / bIIx / I / I //

One Note Samba

The following is a bass line for "One Note Samba" in the key of B♭. Note key changes in the bridge from D♭ to B.

(B♭)   III / bIIIx / II / bIIx / III / bIIIx / II / bIIx / Vm / bV /

(B♭)   IV / bVIIx / III / bIIIx / II bIIx / I^{+6} // (D♭) II / V / I / I //

(B)   II / V / I // (B♭) IIϕ V / III / bIIIx / II / bIIx / III /

(B♭)   bIIIx / II / bIIx / Vm / bV / IV / bVIIx / bIIIM / IIx /

(B♭)   bIIM / I^{+6} //

Just in Time

The following is a bass line for "Just in Time" in B♭.

I / IV / VIIm / IIIx / III / VIx / VI / IIx / II / V / I / Ix / Im^{+6} /

IVx / VII / IIIx / VI / VI$_2$$^{\sharp 7}$ / VI$_2$ / ♭Vø IVm^{+6} / III / VI / VIx$^{\sharp 5}$ /

Vo / ♭Vø / IVm^{+6} / III / ♭IIIx / IIx / II V / I^{+6} / I^{+6} //

Tune-Up

The following is a figured bass for "Tune-Up" in D major. Note modulations.

(D) II / V$^{♭5}$ / I / I^{+6} // (C) II / V$^{♭5}$ / I / I^{+6} // (B♭) II / V /

(B♭) I / VI // (D) II / ♭IIIM / ♭VIM / V / II / V$^{♭5}$ / I / I^{+6} //

(C) II / V$^{♭5}$ / I / I^{+6} // (B♭) II / V / I / VI // (D) II / ♭IIx /

(D) I / I^{+6} //

The Shadow of Your Smile

The following is a bass line for "The Shadow of Your Smile" in the key of G.

pick-up
♭Vø / VIIm / IIIx / VI$^{\sharp 7}$ VI / IIx / II / V / I / IV / VII / IIIx /

VI$^{\sharp}$$^{\sharp 7}$ VI$^{\sharp 7}$ / VI VI$_2$ / ♭Vø / VIIx / IVx / IIIx ♭Vø / VIIm / IIIx /

VI$^{\sharp 7}$ VI / IIx / II / V$^{\sharp 3}$ IVo / IIIø / VIx / II II $\overset{3}{\sharp}$II III / IVm ♭VIIx /

III IIIø / VIx$^{\sharp 3}$ ♭IIIx / IIx / II V$^{\sharp 3}$ / I^{+6} / I^{+6} //

Nica's Dream

The following is a bass line for "Nica's Dream" in b♭ minor. The key series is as follows:

        Bars 1– 6: b♭ minor
        Bars 7–12: G♭ major
        Bars 13–22: b♭ minor
        Bars 23–28: G♭ major
        Bars 29–32: b♭ minor
        Bars 33–46: D♭ major
        Bars 47–54: b♭ minor
        Bars 55–60: G♭ major
        Bars 61–64: b♭ minor

pick-up

(b♭)   ♭IIx // I / I^{+6} / ♭VIImL / ♭VIIm^{+6} / I / I^{+6} // (G♭) II$^{♯♯7}$ /

(G♭) II$^{♯7}$ / II / ♭IIx / I^{+6} / IVx // (b♭) II / ♭IIx / I^{+6} / I^{+6} / I / I^{+6} /

(b♭)   ♭VIImL / ♭VIIm^{+6} / I / I^{+6} // (G♭) II$^{♯♯7}$ / II$^{♯7}$ / II / ♭IIx /

(G♭) I^{+6} / IVx // (b♭) II / ♭IIx / I^{+6} / I^{+6} // (D♭) II / IIϕ /

(D♭) IĪI IĪ Ī ♭VĪIM / VIx$^{♯5}$ / IIx / II ♭IIx / Io / I VI / II / IIϕ /

(D♭) IĪI IĪ Ī ♭VĪIM / VIx$^{♯5}$ / IIx / II II$_2$ // (b♭) IIx / ♭IIx / I / I^{+6} /

(b♭)   ♭VIImL / ♭VIIm^{+6} / I / I^{+6} // (G♭) II$^{♯♯7}$ / II$^{♯7}$ / II / ♭IIx /

(G♭) I^{+6} / IVx // (B♭) II / ♭IIx / I^{+6} / I^{+6} //

NICA'S DREAM—by Horace Silver
    © 1956 Ecaroh Music, Inc. © 1975 Ecaroh Music, Inc.
    Used by permission.

Four

The following is a figured bass for "Four" in E♭ major.

♭IIx // I II / ♯IIo III / Im / IVx / II / III / IVm /

pick-up

♭VIIx / III / ♭III ♭VIx / II II$_2$ / VIIm IIIx / III / ♭III ♭VIx / II / ♭IIx /

I II / ♯IIo III / Im / IVx / II / III / IVm / ♭VIIx / III / ♭III ♭VIx / II II$_2$ /

VIIm IIIx / III ♭III / II ♭IIx / I^{+6} / I^{+6} //

FOUR—by Miles Davis
    Courtesy of Prestige Music Co., Inc.
    Used by permission.

Quiet Nights and Quiet Stars

The following is a bass line for "Quiet Nights and Quiet Stars" in the key of C.

IV$^4_3$ / % / bIIx$^4_3$ / % / Vm / Ix$^{\sharp3}$ / IV / IV / IVm / bVIIx / IIIx$^{\sharp5}$ /

VIx$^{\sharp5}$ / VI / IIx / II II$_2$ / VII bVIIx / IIx$^4_3$ / % / bIIx$^4_3$ / % / Vm /

Ix$^{\sharp3}$ / IV / IV / IVm / bVIIx$^{\flat5}$ / III / VI / II / V$^{\sharp3}$ / IIIϕ / bIIIx / II /

bIIx / I / I^{+6} //

What Are You Doing the Rest of Your Life

The following is a bass line for "What Are You Doing the Rest of Your Life" in (a) minor. The chord chart is scored in C major, although the final cadences occur in the relative minor. Note key changes.

pick-up
(C)   bVIIx // VI$^{\sharp7}$ VI$_2$$^{\sharp7}$ / VI$_2$ bVϕ / IV IV$^{\sharp5}$ / IV^{+6} IV$_2$ /

(C)   II$^{\sharp\sharp7}$ II$^{\sharp7}$ / II II$_2$ / VII / bVIIx / VI$^{\sharp7}$ VI$_2$$^{\sharp7}$ / II II$_2$ / VII /

(C)   bVIIx / VI$^{\sharp7}$ VI$_2$$^{\sharp7}$ / VI$_2$ bVϕ / IV IV$^{\sharp5}$ / IV^{+6} IV$_2$ / II II$_2$ //

(A)   II bIIx / I II / III VI / II bIIx / I VI / II bVIIx / I IV //

(Gb) II bIIx / I I^{+6} // (F) II bIIx / I I$_2$ VI VI$_2$ // (C) VI$^{\sharp7}$ VI$_2$$^{\sharp7}$ /

(C)   VI$_2$ bVϕ / IV IV$^{\sharp5}$ / IV^{+6} IV$_2$ / II$^{\sharp\sharp7}$ II$^{\sharp7}$ / II II$_2$ / VII /

(C)   IIIx VI // (a) IV IV$_2$ / II bIIx / Im / IVx / II / bIIx / I^{+6} / I^{+6} //

Carolina Shout

CAROLINA SHOUT—by James P. Johnson

213

215

216

217

223